DATE DUE

ILL 2/18/19	

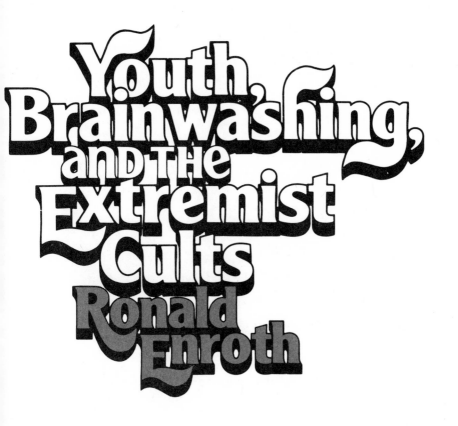

Youth, Brainwashing, and the Extremist Cults

Ronald Enroth

**ZONDERVAN
PUBLISHING HOUSE** OF THE ZONDERVAN CORPORATION
GRAND RAPIDS, MICHIGAN 49506

Library of Congress Cataloging in Publication Data

Enroth, Ronald M
    Youth, brainwashing, and the extremist cults.

    Includes index.
    1. Cults.   2. Youth — Religious life.   I. Title.
BP603.E6   301.5'8   77-5865

Cloth: ISBN 0-310-24270-3
Paper: ISBN 0-310-24271-1

PRINTED IN THE UNITED STATES OF AMERICA

TO MY FAMILY:

My wife, Ruth-Anne
My daughters, Kara and Becky

◆ CONTENTS ◆

◆ ACKNOWLEDGMENTS ◆

NO MATTER what title pages may say, to name one person as the author of a book is less than accurate. There is little in this book that I did not receive from others.

My thanks first and foremost are due to the many young people who willingly and sometimes painfully shared with me their experiences in various cult groups. I have not indicated their names because of my desire to protect their privacy, but without their assistance this book could not have been written.

Many people have helped in this project, but I would like to express special appreciation to Mr. and Mrs. J. C. Crampton, whose selfless dedication to others has not gone unnoticed. For their faithful assistance in typing the manuscript, I wish to thank Susan Martins, Dalene Whitlock, and Jollene Anderson. I am also grateful to the following people who have participated in this endeavor in various capacities: Evan Adams, David Dolan, Michael Woodruff, Brooks Alexander, David Fetcho, Cora Nickel, Jeanine Ostini, Marge van Boven, and Bernice Hogervorst.

Finally, my gratitude is greatest to my wife and children, who patiently understood when I became something of a recluse during the writing of the manuscript.

GRATEFUL appreciation is expressed to the publishers for permission to quote from the following books:

Rosabeth Moss Kanter, *Commitment and Community* (Cambridge, MA: Harvard University Press, 1972).

Francine Jeanne Daner, *The American Children of Krsna* (New York: Holt, Rinehart and Winston, 1976).

◆ INTRODUCTION ◆

Held Captive by a Cult

Two Ex-Cultists Return to Kin, Admit Deception

WAS PSYCHOLOGICALLY KIDNAPED,
SAYS 'RESCUED' MEMBER OF CULT

Religious Group Doesn't Kidnap, Says Its Leader

Krishna: Mind-Control or Religious Freedom?

CULTISTS' WORDS FADE, HARSH MEMORIES REMAIN

Parents Fight Cults to Save Children

BRAINWASHED CULTIST PLACED IN WIFE'S CUSTODY

THE ABOVE sampling of headlines taken during the past five years from newspapers in various parts of the United States typify the many news items and feature articles that signal a dramatic increase in the activities of religious cults in America and abroad. Behind each of these headlines is a story of bizarre behavior that the average person would probably find unbelievable and incomprehensible. In almost every case, there is an element of parental anguish and confusion occasioned by events and processes that frequently approach nightmarish proportions.

11

Nearly all encounters with the cults involve a sequence of experiences and characteristic responses that comprise an almost predictable pattern. In a real sense the familiar expression, Once you've seen one, you've seen them all, is applicable to current cult groups. Yet closer examination reveals an incredible diversity. Each is virtually an island unto itself. The commonality of certain means to certain ends is so striking, however, that one is tempted to conclude that conspiratorial forces are at work. The tactics and techniques seem to be taken from the same mold.

Invariably the victims of the so-called new-age cults are young. Why this is the case will be explored later. They are vulnerable — a trait with tragic implications. They become "true believers" who cluster around authoritarian leaders and attempt to convince the benighted world that they have discovered Truth with a capital *T*.

The hallmarks of cultic conversion usually include the abandonment of a familiar life style; severing of ties with friends and families; a radical and sometimes sudden change in personality; the relinquishing of possessions; indoctrination with a new set of values, goals, and beliefs; the assuming of a totally new identity, including for some a new name; the acquisition of a new "spiritual" family; unquestioned submission to leaders and group priorities; isolation from the "outside world" with its attendant evil; subversion of the will; thought reform; the adoption of new sociocultural and spiritual insignia; and a host of other less dramatic though equally significant characteristics. As we shall see, there are even physiological dimensions to cultic involvement.

This book will consider the whole range of phenomena — sociological, psychological, spiritual — surrounding the emergence and development since 1965 of a growing group of religious new-age cults. More specifically, the book will deal with what might be called the "careers" of cult members. Questions I address myself to include, What type of person is attracted to cults, and why? What are the circumstances surrounding entry into the cults? How are young people recruited? What happens to the person once he/she joins a group? What are some of the behind-the-scenes activities in cult groups? What is the role of leaders? How do young people get out of cults?

Of equal concern are matters such as, What are the implications of cult activity for the church and individual Christians? What can parents do when their children join cults? How do cults secure their funds? What is "deprograming," and why is it controversial? What are some of the theological issues associated with specific groups? Finally, some of the broader questions — and perhaps the most significant ones — relate to how all this demonstrates the influence of the adversary — Satan. Then also we must all evaluate the meaning of increased cult activity for our culture, our families, and our individual lives.

I SPEAK AS a sociologist and as an evangelical Christian. Both perspectives will be evident to the reader, and both are valuable. As a social scientist, I have attempted to conduct the research upon which this book is based in a careful, objective fashion. I do not think it is possible to be a value-free sociologist, however, and that fact undoubtedly emerges in my writing. Unashamedly I admit my bias as an evangelical Christian. I subscribe to the historic, orthodox doctrines of the Christian church, and for that reason attach the label "spiritual counterfeits" to the cult groups described in this volume. To arrive at any other designation would be inconsistent with the position of biblical orthodoxy I value.

Having said that, I am careful to point out that this book is not a theological treatise on the cults. Some readers will undoubtedly be disappointed because the beliefs and doctrinal systems of the various cults are given scant attention. That would be a major undertaking in itself, and I leave that important task to those with the necessary training and knowledge.

The information contained in this book is largely the result of sociological research conducted for more than a year. To obtain as complete a picture of contemporary cults as possible, I conducted in-depth interviews with dozens of former members, as well as parents, relatives, and friends of active cultists and ex-cultists. All interviews were taped. In each case I requested written permission to record our conversations and to use the transcriptions in my research and writing. The actual names of the people I interviewed (whether in person or by cassette tape via the mail) do not appear in the book; they have been changed to protect the anonymity of the participants.

It is probably impossible to estimate with any real accuracy the number of new-age cults currently active in the United States. They number in the dozens. I have selected the most prominent movements as well as a few lesser-known groups for the focus of my study. I sorted out one particular person's story in each of the cult groupings for use in Part 1, "Case Histories From the Cults." I believe these to be reasonably representative case histories.

Throughout the book I have allowed the former members to speak for themselves. In the case histories especially, I have engaged in only minor editing (for the sake of brevity), desiring that the essence of the original discussion be preserved and the informal style of speech and vocabulary be retained.

Another valuable source of data consists of diaries and notebooks kept by members of various groups, copies of letters sent to parents by young people while still in the cults, and publications and other printed materials circulated within groups or distributed to the public.

Part 2 is entitled "Commentary on the Cults" and contains the more analytic and interpretative chapters of the book. The analysis was constructed from the transcriptions of the interviews and the other materials mentioned above and from the related research of other scholars and writers. Throughout the research process, all material was documented from independent sources and confirmed by more than one source whenever possible.

In brief, this book contains the words and statements of others as well as my own analysis and interpretation. I have attempted to write in a readable yet informed manner, utilizing the insights from my academic discipline whenever possible while avoiding dependence on scholarly jargon or emphasizing the exotic. The very nature of the subject easily lends itself to sensationalism, a factor not overlooked in some journalistic accounts. It has not been my purpose to select out the more sensational aspects of cultic activity, though some of the practices and experiences described are clearly unusual from the perspective of mainstream American society.

THE HISTORY of my own academic involvement with the topic goes back to the summer of 1971. I am a student of current religious movements, and at that time I was engaged in research for a book I co-authored, The Jesus People (Wm. B. Eerdmans Publishing Co., 1972). We soon discovered that the Jesus People were not a monolithic movement: they comprised diverse elements. Two groups generally associated with the Jesus movement at the time — the Children of God and the Alamo Christian Foundation — emerged clearly as fringe groups, extremist elements vis-à-vis the mainstream Jesus People.

Accounts of very strange behavior began to filter out of these two groups. Reports of zombie-like personalities, self-hypnosis, mind control, eccentric behavior in both sexual and spiritual realms, and "brainwashing" became increasingly common. Since publication of The Jesus People, I have had conversations with several former members of the extremist groups discussed in that book. As time went on, I encountered more and more people who reported similar experiences but who had been members of groups clearly outside even marginally Christian groups. Young people who had been involved in groups like the Divine Light Mission and the Hare Krishna movement seemed to be telling stories remarkably similar to those of ex-members of the Children of God.

About this same time, a number of grass-roots parents' organizations came into being around the country. Magazines like Time and Newsweek began reporting the legal battles of Ted Patrick, the first and most publicized "deprogramer." I discovered that relatively few people, in or outside the church, knew what was really happening on the cult scene. In an effort to help provide additional carefully researched information, I began my study of youth, brainwashing, and extremist cults. The results are presented in this book.

◆ Part 1 ◆

Case Histories From the Cults

◆ ONE ◆

The Hare Krishna Movement

FOR THE past decade the streets of many American cities have displayed an increasingly common scene: exuberant young men and women dressed in bright, saffron robes — the men with their heads shaved — chanting the holy names of "god": "Hare Krishna, Hare Krishna, Krishna Krishna, Hare Hare, Hare Rama, Hare Rama, Rama Rama, Hare Hare."

On street corners and at airports, these young people, frequently "disguised" in conventional middle-class clothes, sell their movement's books and magazine, *Back to Godhead*. Officially known as the International Society for Krishna Consciousness (ISKCON), the cult was founded by His Divine Grace, A. C. Bhaktivedanta Swami Prabhupada, who first came to the United States in 1965. By October 1966 this Spiritual Master (or guru) had established the Hindu cult of Krishna worship in a small storefront in New York City. The cult's objective is to promote "spiritual enlightenment" and to spread the pure love of God (Krishna) throughout Western society. The devotees of Krishna follow a traditionally ascetic Hindu life style which revolves around an elaborate network of approximately fifty communelike temples in urban areas of the United States. Hare Krishna leaders state that the movement has ten thousand full-time devotees in America and approximately five thousand full-time residents at urban foreign centers the world over.

Lisa Bryant first encountered Hare Krishna people during a visit to San Francisco for a Christmas vacation when she was ten years old. "I remember walking on the streets with my parents, and this really weird girl came up to me and wanted a donation. I had never seen anything like it before and I thought it was strange. But I gave a donation anyway, and she gave me a magazine. After reading the magazine, I concluded they must be crazy.

"The second time I heard about them was after a girl friend had returned from Denver, where she had been stopped by a Hare Krishna and invited to a feast." The young man also gave her the location of a temple near her home in Southern California. Upon returning home, Lisa's girl friend said she wanted to visit the center and asked Lisa to accompany her.

"So we went to Laguna Beach to visit the temple there. My first impression was that these people were absolutely crazy, insane. I thought they were totally flipped out. When we walked inside, the first thing I heard was the sound of coins being counted. I thought to myself, *Listen to all that money they're counting. They're in the business of making money.* At that point in time, I hadn't read anything about them, pro or con. I didn't realize that they were a cult, and I didn't know then how they got their money. But my first impression was that they were a very legitimate organization."

Lisa's friend returned to the group the next day and decided to spend a few nights with them. "When she came back to my house, she was wearing their clothes and the beads and she told me she was going to join them. It was such a shock, because she was my best friend. I admired her a lot because she was older than I, and I couldn't believe that she was going to join them after just three days. I tried to talk her out of it and went with her a few more times to the temple. The more I tried to get her out, the more she pulled me into it. After a few weeks, I was beginning to let down my defenses. I was beginning to feel that some things they did weren't so bad."

Lisa was fourteen then and was clearly on a serious spiritual search. "Nowadays everyone is searching for values and they spoke with authority. It was like meeting someone who said, 'I know the perfect answer to life, the perfect answer for everything.' Whereas my other teachers — confirmation teacher included — were always vague and never answered my questions fully, these people could answer my questions.

"For a long time I had been visiting a lot of different churches, looking for the right one. I was trying to find spiritual peace and happiness and answers to questions like, 'Why am I here, why are persons born with birth defects, why do some people die young?' The Hare Krishnas had answers, whereas other people would say, 'I don't know.' I was looking for some clear-cut answers."

The Krishna devotees persuaded Lisa that her parents represented a bad influence on her life. They were very explicit about the need to leave home and live with them at the temple.

Lisa left home and embarked on an incredible odyssey that was to last more than a year. The adventure was to transform a typical Southern California teen-ager into a chanting advocate of Krishna Consciousness. She stopped wearing make-up, gave some of her possessions to classmates, and received assurances from temple leaders that she would be sent someplace where her parents couldn't find her. Disguised as a pregnant woman, Lisa was placed on a jet bound for New Orleans. As a neophyte devotee, she quickly learned the temple rules and regulations.

THERE ARE four basic rules of conduct which all new members must observe. These rules are crucial to the Hare Krishna life style, as discussed by anthropologist Francine Daner in her book *The American Children of Krsna:*

1. No gambling. This rule also excludes frivolous sports and games. In addition, devotees are advised not to engage in any conversation that is not connected with the teachings of Krsna Consciousness or with the execution of duties. All other speech or reading is called mental speculation and is a luxury in which the devotees do not engage.

2. No intoxicants. This rule includes all narcotics, alcoholic beverages, tobacco, coffee and tea. ISKCON's efficiency in getting its members to abandon the use of drugs such as marijuana, LSD, and others, has drawn commendation from the mayors of New York and San Francisco. Medicines may be taken when absolutely necessary, but whenever possible medicines containing narcotic substances should be avoided. In actual practice, the devotees will see a doctor and take medicine,

but chanting the Hare Krsna mantra is considered to be a better remedy for bodily ills. The devotees feel that bodily ills are Krsna's mercy because the illness reminds them "that they are not this body."

3. No illicit sex. Sexual relations are permitted only between individuals married by a qualified devotee in Krsna Consciousness. There is no dating or courtship allowed. Marriage is an arrangement for two devotees of Krsna to serve and worship in this way. A swami stated it succinctly: "If a devotee believes he can serve Krsna better by being married, then he gets married. Marriage is primarily for the purpose of raising children in Krsna Consciousness."

4. No eating of meat, fish, or eggs. The only food that can be eaten by devotees is food prepared under strict dietary regulations, and offered by prescribed ceremony to Krsna. When traveling or under unusual circumstances, devotees may eat foods such as fruit or milk which can easily be offered and which do not necessarily require preparation; under no circumstances may unoffered food be eaten. In ISKCON, eating is an act of worship and must be conducted accordingly (pp. 60–61).*

Besides learning the importance of strictly observing the four temple rules, the new devotee is taught how to chant, how to participate in the temple ceremonies, and how to prostrate himself before the deities of wood and marble.

Full membership in the cult is attained by stages. The candidate must first enter into temple life (or temple service) for a time to demonstrate his devotion. As one ex-member put it, "You try it on for size and see how it goes." During this pre-initiation stage, the new recruit is called by his first name, never by his last name. Older, advanced devotees stress the importance of making a total commitment to the movement's philosophy. Lisa notes, "It was impressed upon me that if I didn't make such a commitment, there wouldn't be any real way practically for me to escape this earth spiritually. It was a matter of spiritual life and death."

After a devotee has participated in temple service for a period of time, usually six months or more, he/she is eligible for

*This and other quotations are from *The American Children of Krsna: A Study of the Hare Krsna Movement* by Francine Jeanne Daner. Copyright© 1976 by Holt, Rinehart and Winston. Reprinted by permission of Holt, Rinehart and Winston.

initiation. The temple president presides over an elaborate fire ceremony called a *harer-nama*, or holy name initiation. Lisa describes her initiation: "They built a fire in the center of the room, and then they threw seven different kinds of grains on it. Butter was poured on top of it and as it began to smoke, they started to chant. I was given a new spiritual name (a Sanskrit name) and three strands of neck beads." These tiny beads, which Lisa now refers to as "Krishna's dog-collar," are to be worn until the devotee dies.

After an additional waiting period of at least six months, the devotee is eligible for a second rite, the brahminical initiation. "If you have a good record and you do everything you're told to do without questioning and you're faithful in your service, you achieve a state of spiritual advancement. If they think you are sufficiently advanced and devoted to their cause, you can be initiated a brahmin." This second initiation involves, for the men, the receiving of a sacred thread which is worn over the left shoulder and across the chest. Women do not receive a brahminical thread. The devotees are also given a secret mantra, the *gayatri* mantra, which is to be chanted three times a day.

The next step up the spiritual ladder is known as *sannyasa*, a renunciation stage reserved for especially devoted men. It entails a life-long vow of poverty and celibacy and a commitment to preach and do good works. Few attain this stage. Lisa notes, "Whenever devotees see these *sannyasi*, they are supposed to prostrate themselves on the floor, because these monks are considered to be really holy."

The ultimate objective of the Hare Krishna devotee is to be engaged in a life of "loving service" to Krishna, the Supreme Lord. The cult teaches that such selfless service to God, known as *bhakti*, is the path to truth and happiness. In fulfilling that role, man lives a life that is karmically pure by sowing good seeds of good actions and ultimately attaining a form of eternal security in one's karmic bank account.

"Since man was created for service, the senses should be engaged in service to God continually. If you use your feet, it is considered doing a work of God. If you use your eyes, it is for the reading of God's material. The ears are for listening to the stories of truth, of scriptures. In short, there must be total devotion of one's mind, body, soul, and senses to the cause of Krishna Consciousness."

THE TEMPLE president is the single most important person shaping the day-to-day activities of Hare Krishna members. The devotee is required to submit fully to the authority of the temple president, who ultimately must answer to the spiritual master, Prabhupada, and carry out his orders. He must see that the deities are cared for, disputes settled, rules followed, and sufficient funds obtained. He also offers spiritual guidance and is the resident authority on scripture and ceremonial procedures.

Lisa felt that each temple had its own characteristic tone, determined largely by the personality and influence of the temple president. For example, some presidents were known to be stricter than others. "I remember one particular girl had developed a really terrible sore throat. . . . She asked the temple president if she could buy some orange juice for her cold. He said no. A week later he came down with a cold and bought some orange juice for himself."

Marriages are arranged by the temple president. He reportedly can order a devotee to marry or can refuse a request for marriage. Lisa states, "I've known people who really wanted to get married and the leaders wouldn't let them. When a person said, 'I'm leaving because I want to get married,' it was interesting that the leaders immediately agreed to arrange the marriage."

In Lisa's opinion, the leadership discouraged people from getting married because the love relationship of a man and woman might thwart the objectives of the group. "They don't like to get people married. They are anti-love, because their goal is to become detached from all worldly involvement. . . . They hate to have people get married, because after marriage the individual will start to love his wife and will not go to the temple as often. It's also a threat to the group, because when a wife has a child, they lose a worker because she has to take care of the child."

Sex is strictly for purposes of procreation. As one temple president put it, "We believe that sex should not be employed simply for the enjoyment of the senses or as an expression of closeness to one's spouse. The highest expression is in seeing to the other's needs, and the main need is God consciousness. The ultimate lover and enjoyer is God. Helping your mate to a higher realization of God is more of an expression of love than sex."

A couple desiring to have a child is permitted to have sexual relations once a month on a day when conception is most likely to occur. Before engaging in sexual activity, the pair must chant fifty rounds on their japa beads to purify themselves.

In the Krishna Consciousness movement, women are accorded a very subservient status.

> ISKCON women are discouraged from doing anything on their own, so they cannot even walk out of the temple without permission. If they go out to do errands, they are always accompanied by another ISKCON member. A woman who is married should ask her husband's permission to do anything beyond her prescribed temple duties. Ideally, the woman must be completely submissive and a constant servant to her husband. The American women devotees do not seem to be able to live up to the Vedic ideal for women, and this is a constant source of friction between man and wife (Daner, p. 68).

Several individuals known to the writer relate an incident occurring near the Los Angeles temple that illustrates the ISKCON attitude toward women. They report meeting a young man and woman, cult members, who apparently were returning from a day of book and magazine solicitation. The woman, carrying a big satchel of books, was obviously ill; her nose was running, her lips and face were chapped. Asked why he did not carry the books, the man replied, "She wants to carry them." After some additional conversation, he asserted for all to hear, "I own her."

There is strict sex segregation within the temple. Women and children worship on one side of the sanctuary, men on the other. Men and women eat separately. Lisa observes, "The women and the men were not supposed to talk to each other.

They were not supposed to have any contact." Unmarried men and unmarried women sleep in separate rooms in the temple; housing for married couples is sometimes provided in an adjacent apartment building or house. It is not unusual for a couple to resume the celibate life after the wife has become pregnant.

LISA REPORTS that sometimes regional differences distinguish one temple from another. Of one temple in Southern California, Lisa remarks, "There is no other temple anywhere like the Laguna Beach temple. It's both the people and the surrounding subculture. All of the devotees there were practically hippies before they joined the temple. The men let their hair grow long, for example, something you would never see in New York or Detroit. In Hawaii I hear it's even worse. Although I've never been there, I understand that devotees go surfing and play electric guitars."

The New Orleans temple is a large, converted mansion whose windows are covered by protective bars. "It was really a depressing place," Lisa recalls. A typical day would begin about 3 A.M. with the ring of an alarm clock. "I used to get up at 2:30 A.M. when I lived in Canada, because there was only one bathroom, and the women had to use the bathroom before the men. You have to take a shower because the Hare Krishnas have this thing about extreme cleanliness. You sometimes take several showers a day." Devotees are not permitted to use toilet paper, but are required to take a shower after defecating.

"After putting on clean clothes (women wear saris, men wear dhotis), you begin to chant japa, using prayer beads. This is a form of individual chanting, and you would try to get in seven or eight rounds before the service started at 4 A.M. The service lasts for half an hour, and it's followed by additional individual chanting. About six the study hour or class would begin. We studied the Bhagavad-Gita, or sacred scriptures. They would chant in Sanskrit, read a particular verse, and then explain it. Then there would be time for questions. Following the class, there would be a little more time for individual chanting if you wanted or needed it. At about 7:30 we had breakfast. After breakfast we would clean up the dishes and do chores around the temple. By the time we were ready to go out and start the day, it would be about ten in the morning."

The primary daily activity of many devotees is to participate in what is termed *sankirtana*, chanting and singing on the
sidewalks. These daily excursions constitute a form of preaching but they also are a major means for soliciting donations.
While some devotees chant and dance, others engage in fund-
raising by selling *Back to Godhead* magazines. The collecting
and chanting would continue until five or six in the evening,
with a brief lunch break back at the temple.

Although full ISKCON garb is sometimes worn while
fund-raising, Lisa indicates that it is becoming increasingly
common for the devotees to dress in conventional middle-class
clothes, including wigs for the men. "They get better donations
that way." They would often joke about the disguise, according
to Lisa. "They would say, 'Look, we have to dress like *karmis*.'
A *karmi* is a worldly non-member, and so this was a way of
making fun of the other people.

"Each of us would bring in about $60 to $100 per day. We
had to make an individual report. They would say, 'Everyone
count your money.' But we didn't call it money, it was known
as *laksmi*: Laksmi is the Hindu goddess of fortune. We turned
all of the contributions over to the temple leaders and were
never told what happened to the money. You just supposed it
went for things like paying rent and food and transportation.
We brought in a lot of money, but you never really think about
it. Some of the money went to pay for the trips the temple
president would make to India. It would cost $1,000 for a
round-trip just for the plane ticket, and then he would buy a lot
of things for the temple while there.

"Sometimes we would tell people, 'We're feeding people
in India.' "

Hare Krishna members have been known to solicit funds
while dressed up as Santa Claus and the Easter Bunny. During
the American bicentennial celebration, they were reported
seen at Mount Rushmore wearing cowboy hats and proclaim-
ing, "Hi! We're with the Bicentennial Committee. We're raising
money to help sponsor activities in the United States of
America for our two-hundred-year birthday. Would you like to
give a little something?"

After a full day of witnessing and solicitation, the devotees return to the temple about 6 P.M. and shower. "Every time you went out into the streets, you had to take a shower. After getting cleaned up, we would study for thirty minutes or an hour. Then evening services began; they usually lasted thirty minutes after which we attended another thirty-minute Bhagavad-Gita class. We had classes in the morning and classes in the evening. Constant indoctrination. When you are traveling from place to place, they have a tape playing in the van or car, a teaching tape or a chanting tape. Around 8:15 or so we would have hot milk in order to sleep better. We were also told that it supplied valuable brain substance necessary to understand spiritual matters. We would then study until 9 or 10 P.M., but sometimes there were other duties to perform. For example, we would make flower garlands for the idols, the deities. We were usually in bed by 10 P.M. Six hours was the maximum sleep allowed."

The statues of deities found in every ISKCON temple are not considered idols by the devotees, but rather are viewed as incarnations of Krishna appearing in material forms. Lisa comments, "We took very good care of those deities. They were dusted in the morning, dressed, and fed. We bathed them in rose water." Actually the liquid used to bathe the Krishna statue consists of rose water, honey, milk, and a small amount of cow's urine. After completing the ceremony, devotees consider it an honor to drink the liquid.

WHILE LISA was in New Orleans, she had no contact with her parents, who were attempting to locate her. Temple leaders in Los Angeles and Laguna Beach claimed they did not know where Lisa was. Her father placed an announcement and her picture in a New Orleans fire station, offering a $500 reward for information leading to her return. Someone finally recognized Lisa and notified police. Lisa states that temple officials at first hid her from the police, but she was later taken into custody while witnessing.

After being returned to her parents, Lisa remained withdrawn and zombie-like in behavior. Her mother said Lisa was not the "loving and affectionate" daughter she had once known. Three weeks later Lisa rejoined the cult.

Temple authorities in Southern California arranged to send Lisa to a temple in Ottawa, Canada. She was again disguised as a pregnant woman and placed on a jet. "I received royal treatment because most devotees simply don't go flying from here to there. But they were willing to do anything to keep me out of contact with my parents."

Lisa found the living conditions in Ottawa much more favorable than her previous experience in the New Orleans temple. "The president in Canada was very nice. He took better care of your physical needs, like providing clothing and things like that. By comparison, in New Orleans it was terrible."

Whenever she left the Ottawa temple, she was required to wear a wig so that no one could recognize her in case her parents were circulating photos of her. During this time, her parents were indeed working with Canadian police. After receiving a tip from a girl friend who had received a letter from the sixteen-year-old devotee, Lisa's father drove to Ottawa and demanded that temple leaders produce his daughter. They denied that she was there. Bryant then notified immigration officials that his daughter was an illegal alien. They obtained a search warrant and laid plans to look for her. While this was happening, the police visited the temple and as soon as Lisa saw them, she went out the back door and was put into hiding at a little farm. She remembers being all alone in the farmhouse and thinking, "No one in the world knows where I am except these people. What if something happened and they tried to get rid of me? I was in an isolated farmhouse, no neighbors for miles around, and it really scared me. They could have killed me, buried me in a hole by the house, and no one would have known."

In desperation, Lisa's father took her photograph to the businesses in the vicinity of the Ottawa temple. All the merchants recognized her and were willing to affirm in court that she lived in the area. The temple president persisted, however, in denying that he had any knowledge of Lisa's whereabouts.

The Hare Krishna people had other plans for Lisa. "They wanted to get me married because in Canada, at age sixteen, you can legally marry without your parents' consent." A snag developed, however, since proof of Canadian citizenship was required. Lisa is an American citizen.

The devotees went all-out to protect Lisa from any polluting contact with her parents. They had her write a letter to her mother and father stating that she no longer was with the Hare Krishnas, but instead was traveling in Mexico with a group of musicians. The message amounted to "I don't want to come back home. I'm having a wonderful time."

With the letter went a photograph of Lisa standing beside an unidentified body of water with three young men and one woman — all obviously countercultural in appearance. These were her purported hippie traveling companions. The letter also communicated that after she had quit the Krishnas, Lisa happened to meet someone who used to eat at the ISKCON temple in New Orleans. He told her that her parents had been "molesting" the Krishna people. So she was now asking her parents to "leave them alone" since, after all, she was no longer a part of their organization.

Mrs. Bryant was suspicious of the letter at the outset. The photo clearly showed Lisa wearing the cult's beads — the Krishna "dog-collar." Also, the wording of the letter was not in Lisa's normal style of writing: the word patterns seemed too much like ISKCON phrasing. Yet, the letter bore a Mexican postmark.

Another similar letter from Lisa, also with a Mexican postmark, was received soon thereafter by the president of the Laguna Beach temple. He promptly telephoned a local police captain who had been working with Lisa's parents and shared his news: "This proves that Lisa is not in our temple any longer; she's traveling with musicians somewhere."

At first the police viewed the story as plausible. But Lisa's parents kept going back to the police and voicing their reservations. Finally the police joined them in concluding that the story was a hoax.

Later it was learned that the photograph had been posed — in front of a lake in Ottawa. The letters had been written by a fellow devotee who had concocted the whole deceptive strategy; Lisa was then asked to copy the letters, and they were forwarded to a Mexican temple for mailing inside Mexico. The young man who had devised the scheme was so proud of what he had accomplished that he showed the photo to a girl friend of Lisa in New Orleans. Subsequently this friend left the movement, met Lisa's parents, explained the photo hoax to them, and confirmed that their daughter was in Ottawa.

While she was living in Canada, Lisa's faith in the organization remained unshakable. She regarded her parents and friends in the world as merely "flesh relationships," outsiders, *karmis*. She would say to herself, "Look at these poor *karmis*. They're out there, and all they know is that they have to get up in the morning to go to work. They try to make a buck so they can have a little pleasure. When they come home, their family doesn't respect them, their wives are equal to them, they don't have any feeling of superiority, and their children don't respect them. Just look at these poor people. If I sell them a book, they'll just be so happy."

The devotees relegated all parents to the category of *karmis*. Some parents, however, were more cooperative and less threatening to the organization's goals. If they didn't object to their child's activities, if they didn't make waves, they were viewed as "pious" parents. But, as Lisa observes, "If your parents were like my parents and caused a big scene, they were demons."

Lisa's parents were determined to retrieve her from the cult. After Lisa had eluded the police and her father in Ottawa, Bryant returned to the United States. He continued to pressure ISKCON officials and reminded them of a letter Lisa had written to her girl friend which mentioned some of the activities going on behind the scenes. Some of the ISKCON leaders became increasingly concerned about the legal implications of the letter. They decided to send Lisa back to Los Angeles to find out if her girl friend still had the letter.

Lisa tells what happened: "The temple president was driving me across Canada to Detroit, where I was to get on the plane. Before crossing the border into Detroit, he stopped and phoned a regional director for instructions. The official told him, 'I don't want you to take her across the border. It's too dangerous; you could get caught and you could get arrested. Just leave her there and let her get across on her own. She can get to L.A. on her own.' That just blew my mind! Most leaders would have followed such direct orders, but this president was a little nicer than most, and he realized that he just couldn't abandon me. So he drove me across the border.

"Once we got into the U.S., he put me on a plane in Detroit."

THE TRIP proved to be a turning point in Lisa's Hare Krishna pilgrimage. "When I was on the plane, I had a really emotional experience, because I came to the realization that they were in fact kicking me out. For over a year now, they had protected me, flown me, hidden me, lied for me. I thought it was because I was so devoted, because I really believed. I was considered advanced for being in the organization only a year.

"When I got on that plane, I realized the implications of what they wanted me to do. They wanted me to go with a West Coast leader to an attorney and make a statement and then turn myself in to the police. They asked me to tell the police that I didn't want to go home to my parents, but would rather be placed in a foster home. I later realized that they were fearful that my parents might influence me to take them to court. They wanted me to make a legal statement that I was never forced to do anything and that they didn't know my actual age. Also, they wanted to have me take psychiatric tests to prove that I wasn't crazy at the time I left home.

"As soon as I got in the plane and realized what was happening, I cried and cried. I had been dependent on them for everything, and now I knew I had to go back into the regular world, return to a regular life style and I didn't want to. All I wanted to do was to be a devotee. The whole time I was in the movement I was told that it would be impossible to go back to that life, to go back where you left off. They said it was like eating vomit. I had been conditioned to think that way, and now this is what they were doing to me. They were forcing me to do this."

Lisa was met by devotees in L.A. "One of the persons to greet me was a short lady about thirty-five years old who had been in the movement for five years. She became my body-guard. All of the sudden I was a prisoner, a literal prisoner. If I said I had to go to the bathroom, she said, 'So do I.' If I said, 'I'm going for a little walk to chant the rest of my rounds,' she would join me. No matter what I did, she was by my side."

The devotees were attempting to persuade Lisa not to make trouble for the Krishna leaders. She had one frightening experience when a member of the group, a very large man, grabbed the woman who was guarding Lisa and pulled her aside. "It was unusual that he would even touch a woman. I heard him say under his breath, 'Are you watching that girl? You're not letting her get away, are you?' I had never seen anything like that before, and I was really scared. This is when the wheel slowly started to turn. I was forced to think, *What am I going to do? Am I going to do what they want me to do, or am I going to go back home to my parents?* At that point I think I became schizophrenic, because half of me was a devotee wanting very much to be a true believer while the other half of me was saying, 'These people are nuts.'

"We slept on the floor, in sleeping bags. I can remember lying awake at night sensing that the woman assigned to guard me was also awake. I remember having intense headaches, because I had been thinking all night long, wondering what I was going to do. One morning my guard got sick and she fell asleep. I was taking a shower, and when I stepped out of the shower, I saw that she was sleeping. The other people who lived in the apartment were also gone, and so I knew that this was my opportunity. I grabbed my things and ran out the door. I was really scared, because the whole street was a Hare Krishna neighborhood. There were Hare Krishna people living in every apartment house, and I thought, *Even if I run down the street, they will all come after me and that will be it.* I took a short-cut and ran out onto Venice Boulevard, and only a few people saw me. I ran just as fast as I could. I was still confused and scared, but I had seen enough to know that they really didn't care about me and my spiritual advancement. If they had cared, they wouldn't have done what they did. I hitchhiked to a friend's house, and she talked me into going back to my parents. So the next morning I walked home."

What followed was several months of gradual readjustment to normal society. Lisa began to read women's magazines

— magazines considered very worldly by the movement. It took her a while to rediscover what was going on in the world of clothes and fashions. Lisa regained interest in mirrors and caring for her hair: she never saw mirrors in Krishna temples. In the movement, the human body is seen as an obstacle to reaching self-realization. Devotees have little regard for their bodies and spend as little time as possible in matters pertaining to clothing and personal appearance.

"After four months, I still had doubts and sometimes thought, *Maybe they are right.* It probably would have taken me longer to return to normalcy, but the thing that helped me immensely was Ted Patrick's book, *Let Our Children Go!* When I read that, I started to cry and cry because it was so true. I had gone through it all myself. I was crying for myself and my own pain, but I was also crying for the people in the book and all the kids who are in the cults. After I read that book, I saw the Hare Krishna movement in a much wider perspective and realized that all of the cults are saying the same thing."

Lisa had attended high school for only two months before joining the Krishna cult. Upon her return, she passed a proficiency test and is now enrolled in college, hoping to pursue a career in interior design. As far as religion is concerned, Lisa admits, "I've had an overdose, and I'm not going to be concerned with it right now."

◆ TWO ◆

The Children of God

JANICE EVANS left home at seventeen. "I felt that I wanted to go out and see the world and discover who I was. I was at the stage when I thought that I knew everything and my parents knew nothing. I was very stubborn and radical. I went out West and didn't see my parents for almost two years. As time went on, I felt that I didn't know my parents anymore. I just couldn't relate to them, although I did write them letters and talk to them on the telephone. If I was ever in trouble, like if I needed money or if I was really down and out, I would never have told them. I didn't want them to worry, and I figured that my problems were my own. That was the case when I landed in Hawaii with only fifteen dollars to my name. I didn't know anybody and I was alone."

Jan first learned of the Children of God when she was living on the island of Hawaii. She was twenty years old then, and she had never heard of them before. "One night one of the guys from COG came to the door of a house I was staying at and talked to us for a little while. I was pretty high that first time I met him, smoking pot and drinking rum. I really thought it was a big joke, as a matter of fact. I asked him questions just to make him look silly. But he had answers to all my questions.

"The thing that attracted me to the Children of God was that they seemed so happy and positive. They were just really full of love, and it was obvious that they really loved me and they cared for me. They were really happy, and that's what I wanted.... Many times they would just leave me completely mystified, because I didn't understand where they were coming from. But they intrigued me, and I continued to listen to them, even though at first I thought they were really jerks, Jesus freaks. I laughed at them. But then I saw them everywhere. I'd walk downtown and I'd see these same two guys and we'd talk. They would even show up at the bar where I worked as a cocktail waitress just to say hello and see how I was doing. It was amazing. Everytime I turned around there they were.

"After a couple of days they needed a place to stay, so I let them stay at my apartment. But my landlord knew who the Children of God were, and he became really worried about me and told me that he did not want them to stay in the apartment. Because of my landlord's negative attitude towards the Children of God, I was even more attracted to them, because I thought my landlord was a jerk as it was, anyway. I really didn't believe my landlord because he was mean to me and these guys were nice to me. I didn't see why I should believe somebody who was not very nice to me.

"For about a week and a half I saw them every day; every minute that I wasn't at work I was with them. It just happened that they knew my schedule, and they were always where I was. They talked to me, and we read out of the Bible, which was something that I'd never been interested in. We just talked and did things I liked to do, like walked in the woods. They were very agreeable, and whatever I wanted to do was fine with them. They were just very kind and talked to me and answered all my questions. And that's how, I guess, they recruited me."

THE CHILDREN of God was founded in the late sixties by David Brandt Berg, one-time Bible teacher and itinerant evangelist. Berg spent his early years traveling with his parents, who were evangelists associated with the Christian and Missionary Alliance. After World War II, Berg fell out with leaders of the church he was pastoring. He dropped out of the organized church with feelings of bitterness and contempt for institutionalized religion. He remained persuaded, however, that God had chosen him for some yet-to-be-revealed mission. At the urging of his mother, former radio evangelist Virginia Brandt Berg, he came to Huntington Beach, California, in 1968 to work with the hippies and drug freaks.

Preaching a strongly apocalyptic gospel and attacking the materialistic, individualistic American society with its coldly conventional churches, Berg began to attract a small following of street people, surfers, and assorted dropouts who were willing to "forsake all" to follow this new prophet and his family. After receiving a prophecy that California was about to slide into the sea as a result of an earthquake, Berg left the state with a group of about fifty disciples. For several months, Berg and his band traveled across the United States and Canada, witnessing and demonstrating as they wandered. It was during this period that they began calling themselves the Children of God, and their leader — now known as "Mo," or Moses David — began to formulate the group's unique program and structure. Berg also took a trip to Europe and Israel to explore possibilities for establishing colonies or communities abroad. Increasingly Berg segregated himself from his growing following and interacted primarily with the movement's highest leaders, which included some of his own children.

In early 1970, some 120 Children of God were given permission to use facilities in Texas and California owned by TV evangelist Fred Jordan. The Jesus People movement was by this time a much-publicized addition to the American religious scene. Jordan provided appropriately conservative clothes for some of the COG and effectively used the testimonials and songs of the smiling converts on his TV programs. A rupture in the relationship between Jordan and the Children soon developed, and he evicted them from his properties in September 1971. From a membership of approximately 500 at that time, the COG has expanded to an estimated 4,000 full-time members currently organized into over 400 colonies throughout the world.

AFTER A WEEK and a half of witnessing to Jan, the COG disciples received word from the island of Oahu, where the main colony was located, that they had to return home. "There was going to be a big rock music festival, and the Children of God were planning to set up a booth for the distribution of free food," Jan relates. "They asked me if I would care to come along and help them set up this free food booth. At that time I had absolutely no idea how they lived and what they were really into. Also, it just so happened that I had to be out of my apartment just a couple of days after they were planning to leave. I didn't have another place to go, so I figured I might as well go with them. I'd never seen Oahu and these were nice people and I had no ties where I had been living. I'd only been there a month and I hadn't really made friends with many people.

"The period when I first joined the COG is almost like a fog to me. It's almost like a dream. It was so unlike me to follow other groups, because basically I'm an independent person. But they had a way of applying spiritual explanations to everything that happened. Whenever anything would happen to me, they would say that God was trying to speak to me, to tell me something. For example: I like to fix bicycles, and one time I repaired a bike for this guy, and I wanted to take it for a test drive to see if the gears were shifting properly. One of my friends in the COG said to me, 'You'd better pray before you get on that bike.' I laughed at him. I asked, 'Why should I pray before I get on this bike?' He said, 'I'm serious. You should pray.' So, laughing under my breath, I just said, 'Lord, protect me while I'm on this bicycle. Amen.' I got on the bike and went up the street, and sure enough, I fell off the bike. I used to race bikes, and I don't usually fall off a bike for no apparent reason. And there was no apparent reason why I fell off, but I did."

It was late at night when Jan arrived at the colony in Oahu. "I just laid out my sleeping bag and went to sleep. In the morning I woke up and thought, *Oh boy, I'm really going to be intimidated with all these people around; I don't know anything about the Bible or Jesus.* But they were so full of love. When I got up, everybody just threw their arms around me and told me how much they loved me and that they were glad to see me there. They made me feel very accepted and very loved. One girl said, 'I prayed for a new sister to come, and you're the answer to my prayer.' All these little things added up and made me believe that this was really where I was supposed to be. I guess it was just the lack of love, friendship, and acceptance which led me into the hands of these people.

"So after a couple of days of being there, they asked me if I wanted to join the Children of God. I said yes, with the idea that it would not be a lifetime thing. I just thought, *Oh, sure, I'll join this group and see what's going on.* Since I was confused as it was, I thought that this was the right thing to do."

In joining, Jan had to sign a paper turning over all her money and possessions to the Children of God. She did it willingly, for she had little. Her only valuable possessions were a bicycle, a down sleeping bag, and a backpack.

When a young person joins the Children of God, he/she signs this statement: "I promise to give all my goods and income, let you open my mail, obey rules and officers." That statement is part of a much larger application form in which the COG describe themselves as "revolutionary Christian nomads" who are "bypassing the hopeless, unresponsive, older generation and churchy people and bringing 'new-time religion' to a new 'Now Generation'!" The statement continues: "We have declared War of the Spirit on the System's Godless schools, Christless churches, and heartless Mammon! We long to return to the Truth, Love, Peace, and Beauty of our Ancients in dress, customs, appearance, and the simple Life of True Happiness in God and love for our fellow man!"

The would-be revolutionary is forewarned that the rules of the revolution are strict: "Do not leave anywhere without permission, and absence from Bible Study, duties, or witnessing must be only for emergencies by direct permission of the officer in charge. Absence without leave will be considered desertion of your post. You will only be given one warning, after which your place will be given to someone more deserving. 'He sent them out two by two' — you will never go alone, and always a veteran with trainee."

The application form also promises the "revolutionary" that the daily schedule is rigidly controlled: "Unusual circumstances or assignments can change this at a moment's notice, without complaint. The only things you can be sure of are the Lord, hard work, suffering, constant change, and joy. There are no days off, except some Saturdays, or special days, and that usually without meals."

JAN SOON discovered that it is very unrevolutionary to have doubts and to disagree with the leaders. "I couldn't say things or do things that I wanted to do, things that were natural to me. I couldn't ask the question, Why? They wouldn't let me go outside by myself. I just wanted to go outside and breathe fresh air because I really love to be outdoors; but they wouldn't let me go anywhere without another brother or a sister being with me. And I couldn't understand that. They explained it to me by saying that the devil would be right there to try to dissuade and distract me. So they would never let me be alone.

"I didn't always feel like smiling and laughing and loving people. Sometimes I woke up and I was in a bad mood. But in the COG, you couldn't be in a bad mood. You had to always be happy, and if you were feeling down, you had to cover up and make like nothing was wrong so that you didn't influence your brothers or sisters and make them 'stumble,' as they would say. You had to just always be really happy. That didn't seem normal to me. It was like suppressing my real feelings."

A week after Jan joined the Children of God, she developed scabies, a skin disorder accompanied by a persistent itch. "I was confined in a little room for two weeks. I couldn't see anybody. Nobody would come in the room with me. People just handed me food through the door. I couldn't talk to anybody. I had to stay in that room and read Mo letters and read the Bible. Occasionally someone would talk to me through the door. It was really a sad time for me, and it's still hard for me to talk about it today."

When prayer and fasting did not resolve the problem, Jan was eventually given an ointment from a free clinic.

Anyone in the larger society who was not a member of the COG, or who was not sympathetic with its goals and objectives, was classified as a "Systemite." These servants of Satan were described as "rotten, decadent, decrepit, hypocritical, self-righteous, inflexible, affluent, self-satisfied, proud, stubborn, disobedient, blind, blood-thirsty, godless, dead, selfish, churchy, and unchangeable." As Jan describes it, "If you weren't with the Children of God, then you weren't in God's will. You were a robot, a Systemite. You were of the outside world. These kinds of people were thought to have no spiritual consciousness whatsoever. They just had blinders on them, they couldn't see what was going on.

"They completely cut me off from the outside world. I was not allowed to go anywhere without a brother or a sister. I couldn't talk to anyone who was being negative. For example, when I was out 'litnessing' (a COG term which means witnessing by handing out Mo's literature), if someone would say, 'Hey, what are you doing with the Children of God? Don't you know that it's screwed up?' I immediately had to turn away from them and say, 'See you later.' They were supposed to be the devil, and I had to turn away from the devil and rebuke the devil.

"When I wrote to my parents, I had to give my letters to my shepherd, the person immediately over me in my little colony. He read the letters, and if he thought that they were too strong, he would point out things that were wrong and ask me to do it over. They never really told you to do anything, they merely 'suggested' that you do this or that. I had no correspondence with any of my friends, but I did write to my family — my sisters and my brother and my parents. They told me I could write to my friends if I wanted to, but if they wrote back and weren't happy that I was in the COG, then I was not to write to them again. I was just to cut them off because they refused the Word of God, and God would have to deal with them from that point on. You attempted to give them the Word of God and they refused it; therefore God would just have to take care of them in His own way.

"However, if they would send any money or any material things to me, that was okay, because that was one of the ways God could use them for our benefit, for His benefit. They always asked us to write letters to friends and family and ask for money.

"When I signed over all my possessions to them, they had me indicate what my father did for a living, how much money he made, and how rich he was, what kind of possessions he owned, etc., so that they could have that information in their files. One time I told them, 'I can't ask my father for money. He just doesn't have that kind of money to give me.' They said, 'Oh, come on. He owns a business. You can ask him for money. He's got plenty of money.' They would always try to get money from my parents. Since parents represented the devil, the devil might as well help out as much as possible. That's the way they reasoned it."

Moses David early discovered that it was to his advantage to nurture the good will of sympathetic businessmen and parents. The term *kings* was sometimes applied to all those individuals who provided financial support and defended the COG against its opposition. An organization, THANKCOG, was formed, consisting of parents who were favorably disposed to the Children of God and who could counter the position of FREECOG, a group of parents determined to free their children from the Children of God.

When Janice Evans joined the Children of God, she was told she was now part of God's Family. Obedient children were not to make waves. "You could never outwardly say anything against the Children of God to anyone in the Family. It was especially bad to voice a doubt or complaint to a younger brother or sister — younger in terms of spiritual reality. A negative expression was considered a 'murmur,' and a murmur was against God. . . . Doubts and murmurs were just absolutely not tolerated.

"With regard to Moses David, the influence that he has over this group is incredible. If he said for everyone to go and jump off a bridge, three times a day, everyone would do it, three times a day, without question. He is the voice of God; he is the mouthpiece of God for the present age. Just as there were many mouthpieces of God down through the ages, Moses David is considered to be right up there in the line with Moses of the Old Testament.

"When I first started talking to the Children of God, I asked them, 'Who is this guy, Moses David?' They'd say, 'He's just this guy, he's just one of us. He just writes these letters to us and tells us what he thinks.' I would ask, 'How important is this guy to the Children of God?' 'Oh, he's not important at all,' they'd say. 'He doesn't mean anything. He's just a nobody. It's God that's important.' Which is what I wanted to hear, because had they said anything different, I would have had reservations about them. But they handled those early questions very well.

And then when I realized what an important figure he really was in the group, it completely baffled me. I couldn't understand who he was in reference to the group."

MOSES DAVID remains a shadowy figure in self-imposed seclusion someplace outside the United States, probably in Europe. Although he has reportedly delegated much of the day-to-day operation of the world-wide network of colonies to trusted underlings, his influence as founder-leader-prophet remains unchallenged. His primary means of communication with the far-flung faithful (most of whom have never seen him) is the Mo letter. Many of these contain Berg's unique brand of Bible teaching, including his supposedly direct revelations from God concerning the present and future world events. Three letters issued in 1973 warned of impending disaster for the United States in the form of the comet Kohoutek. Berg prophesied, "This could be the end of Fascist America and its new Nazi emperor, and the beginning of the new day for the whole world!"

Some of Mo's so-called sex letters — complete with suggestive artwork — have caused problems for the COG who attempt to peddle them to the public for a donation. Titles like "Sex Works!" "In the Beginning — Sex!" and "Come on, Ma! Burn Your Bra!" have led many to conclude that Berg is preoccupied with sex. Moses David responds to this charge by quoting Scripture: "To the pure, all things are pure." And he adds: "May God damn every self-righteous sex-condemning truth-hiding hypocrite who would hide the truths and beauties of God's creation from his holy pure-minded children!" Berg observes: "We have a sexy God, and a sexy religion, and a very sexy leader with an extremely sexy young following. So, if you don't like sex, you'd better get out while you can."

Other Mo letters are far less controversial and much more mundane. Jan describes one such letter, entitled "The Health Revolution," as "absolutely absurd." She relates an incident involving this particular Mo letter that illustrates the significance attached to the words of Moses David by his followers. "In 'The Health Revolution' he was telling us how we didn't need to brush our teeth. We only needed to rinse our mouth out with water and rub our finger over our teeth every day. It was only necessary to brush your teeth with toothpaste every three or four days. Toothpaste was something that you didn't really need. He also said that dental floss was bad for your teeth and advised us not to use dental floss."

Jan kept on using dental floss, even though Moses David said not to. One day her shepherd saw her using it and rebuked her for it. Jan replied, "Well, Mo himself said you didn't have to follow this letter to the tee, but to do what you thought was right for you." He walked away.

"A couple of days later, he again saw me using dental floss, and he was astounded. He could not believe that I went against Mo and was using dental floss on my own, without even asking him first if I could. He mentioned it again to me, and said, 'You shouldn't use dental floss. I'm suggesting that you don't use it. I'd pray about it before I did it if I were you.'

"You had to pray before you did anything! . . . While taking a shower or cleaning the vegetables or washing the dishes, you were supposed to give the glory to God. That was the big thing, giving all the glory to God and not to yourself."

In the early days of the Children of God movement, the letters from Moses David were written solely for the leaders of the colonies. Many of these eventually got into the hands of people outside the movement and became a source of some embarrassment to the leadership structure because of the language and contents of the missives. Subsequently many letters were made available for public consumption, and literature distribution became a major source of income for the COG. Over 350 letters have been produced thus far.

One such letter, entitled "Explosion," outlines the organizational structure of the Children of God as of May 1975. (For a description of the early days of the COG when the movement was organized into tribes patterned after those of ancient Israel, see Enroth, Ericson, and Peters, *The Jesus People*, 1972.) Apparently Berg felt the need to restructure the leadership patterns and to divide the existing colonies into much smaller units. This, of course, resulted in a rapid increase in the number of colonies. The new rules implemented in 1975 require that no colony have more than twelve members.

In a paper entitled "Observations on the Children of God," Prof. Roy Wallis summarizes the current organizational structure of the Children of God:

> The international structure of COG is presented as a theocracy, with God revealing through King David, i.e., Mo, the directions to be followed by the movement. Berg is supported by his Royal Family of offspring and their spouses, who are the rulers of this New Nation. Members of the Royal Family also occupy good positions in the Council of Ministers with the overall responsibilities of particular activities and a Prime Minister in general direct charge. Below the Council of Ministers are the Bishops. The world has been divided into 12 major areas, with a Bishop responsible for each. Below them are the Regional Shepherds, then the District Shepherds, then the Shepherds for particular colonies (p. 10).

JAN DESCRIBES the colony with which she was associated: "I lived in a house in Hawaii on the island of Oahu with about thirty people, which was an exceptionally large colony. Actually there were six colonies in the one house, since Mo wouldn't permit a colony to be over twelve people.

"When you first entered into the Family, you were called a 'babe.' After three months you were in LT, which means leadership training. But after that you were a leader. You could stay a leader for five years, or you could go on to become a shepherd or a colony shepherd or a district shepherd and so forth on up the ladder. The way you attained a leadership position was by being what they wanted you to be — never complaining, doing the things they wanted you to do.

"We all felt like we were a part of one big family. We referred to each other as 'brothers' and 'sisters,' and when you saw a brother or a sister you greeted them with a hug and a kiss on the cheek. We all did everything together. We'd take turns cooking, and we'd all clean the house at the same time. Everyone awakened at the same time in the morning and went to bed at the same time at night. Everybody was always very beautiful and loving.

"We always used to say that no matter where you are — all over the United States or all over the world — if you ever meet a brother or sister, they'll be the same as you. They'll have the same goals and feelings that you have. At first this was hard for me to relate to, but one day while walking down Waikiki, I met another Children of God that I had never met before, and it was true — they *did* have the same thoughts and expressions. We were all alike, we did everything the same — little Moses David robots. We would read the Bible together in the morning, and we'd eat together. We did virtually everything together except when we went out into the streets collecting money and litnessing, which we always did in two's. So we were never alone.

"We would have big get-togethers down at the park near Waikiki and we'd sing, hold hands, and dance. Frequently we would do a kind of gypsy dance in which two people would hold hands and swing each other around. There were colony meetings which everyone attended. Each person in the colony had assigned duties to perform, which made you feel like you belonged."

Despite the obvious sexual orientation of some of the Mo letters, new disciples are warned that there will be ". . . no smoking or smooching other than 'greeting one another with a holy kiss' — and absolutely no dating." Jan was told that sex was not permitted except for those who were married "in the eyes of God." "As time went on," she says, "I realized that this rule was not as strongly enforced as I thought it was. In practice it was more like whatever the Spirit led you to do, that was all right to do. If God told you in a dream or while you were praying that it was okay for you to sleep with your sister, then you could go to bed with her with God's permission.

"Dating wasn't allowed while you were a 'babe.' After three months you were permitted to date, but only with the permission of your leaders. If you found that you were attracted to a certain person, you had to talk to your leader, and he'd tell you that he would pray about it. And you would have to pray about it, too, of course. If the leaders thought it was okay, they'd agree to let you date a particular person.

"Marriage was simply defined as sleeping with somebody or having intercourse with somebody. If you slept with somebody, then you were married to that person. There was no formal ceremony in the Children of God when two people wanted to get married. We would just have a party, and then they would sleep together. From that time on, they were considered married.

"We always prayed together in the morning. That was the first thing we did when we woke up. We all got together in the living room and held hands and prayed together. Sometimes we stood in a circle and put our arms around each other. At certain times we would have communion and break bread and drink wine together."

JANICE WAS aware of very clear levels or degrees of spirituality within the group. "One of the top leaders, Caleb [members assumed biblical, usually Old Testament, names upon joining the group], was considered to be almost right next to God, because he was right next to Mo and Mo was right next to God. He was so holy I was afraid to talk to him. There were some people in the group that were just so high on the spiritual ladder that they were almost unreachable. I was too humble to even approach them."

New disciples were shielded from negative information about the group that was circulating on the "outside." Jan recalls, "I wasn't allowed for a long time to read anything bad that was written or said about the Children of God. There was an article in *Reader's Digest* that contained just a couple of paragraphs about the Children of God. That particular issue happened to be in the colony and I picked it up. I wanted to read it and see what was being said. But I was not allowed to even go near that magazine because, I was told, it would just fill my mind with garbage. There was no reason for me to have to read that. I was told that I should be reading a Mo letter.

"They would tell you in their own words sometimes what a newspaper or outside group said about the Children of God. They would just laugh and tell you how it wasn't so and that it was all just a big lie. Of course, they never let me read it myself. They'd just explain it to me.

"I never saw anyone physically punished in the COG. You were just brought aside and talked to. You were never embarrassed in front of the whole group. They always just took you aside, and if something was wrong, they'd talk to you about it and tell you to pray about it. The leaders said they too would pray about it, and then you'd get together again the next day and talk about it some more. Usually by then, it would be straightened out, mainly because of the power of suggestion. Whatever they would suggest, that's what you would come up with. . . . They would keep you in line by spiritualizing every- thing. For instance, one time I had a fever and had to be put in isolation. Our leader would come down and tell me that I'd better pray about what was wrong, 'cause obviously God had given me this sickness for a reason. 'You'd better get in contact with God and find out what He wants to teach you.'

"There's absolutely no individual sense of privacy or uniqueness possible in the Children of God. Everyone is the same — out of the same mold that Moses David put you into. Everyone has to have the same goals. That's the reason the organization works so well: there's a real sense of unity. Every- thing was done in groups. There was no privacy. I slept in a bedroom shoulder to shoulder with many girls." Another ex- member observed, "We had to give up our total freedom — even our appearance. I just simply stayed away from mirrors."

AS WITH most cult groups, financial factors concerning the COG are hard to come by. Members are not permitted to hold "systemite" jobs, and the COG are not involved in auxiliary enterprises such as farming and the sale of craft items to pro- vide a financial base for the colonies. Some money is obtained when wealthy new converts join the group and "forsake all." However, most new recruits have few assets to forsake.

Some financial support is derived from individuals and organizations outside the COG who are sympathetic with their objectives. Food stuffs are frequently "provisioned" or "pro- cured" from local supermarkets. This is an example of what the COG call "spoiling Egypt."

Literature sales appear to be the primary source of income at present. Journalist Thomas Moore observes that the income from litnessing is "more than enough to support in style the most corrupt of false prophets." He notes:

> On an average, from what I saw, each member gets out his
> or her quota of 2,000 pieces of literature a week at an

average of ten cents each. That's about $200 a week — more than a lot of kids their age earn as mechanics or secretaries or even reporters. The Staten Island colony, one of the most profitable for litnessing, gets out up to 40,000 Mo letters a week, taking in about $4,000. That adds up to $200,000 a year. . . . That's a lot of untaxable spare change. And only God — and maybe Moses David — knows where it all goes (*New Times,* October 1974).

Jan and her fellow disciples kept careful daily records of the number of people they witnessed to, the number of Mo letters sold, the total number of pieces of literature distributed, the number of hours spent litnessing and witnessing, and the number of converts brought into the fold. "I have never worked so hard in all my life as when I worked collecting money for those Mo letters. I would literally run from person to person. I wouldn't eat lunch just to make more money. Sometimes I would be so tired I would practically fall over. But I wouldn't think of stopping."

Jan was given an extensive list of "Litnessing Tips," designed to assist the neophyte in getting out "the lit." Here are some excerpts from that list:

If a person refuses the lit, let them know you really want them to have it. Tell them it's really good, or it is really heavy, and even that they can have it free. This often turns hearts and results in a donation.

Watch out for extended mirrors on sides of trucks.

Eat enough food so you don't space out and can keep your mind on litnessing.

Go ape! Go till it hurts! — and even when it hurts. Go like mad for Jesus!

When at a concert or a high school and kids are moving fast, it often helps to shorten your speech to "Can you help with change for kids?" or "Any change for kids?"

If some people are trying to discourage you and bring you down, remember what Mo said: "If you do it the right way the devil will fight you. If you're never getting any objections you must not be doing the job."

Eye contact is very important. Give 'em a look of love and watch their hearts turn. Watch your breath! Be sure to brush your teeth and use mints. You can blow away a lot of potential "givers."

Don't get hung up on people who want lengthy explanations before they feel led to give a donation. Keep moving! And remember, the guy behind him is probably willing to give a dollar for a good cause.

System shirts and bright clothing instead of worn out blue jeans and army jackets will not only lift your spirit, but will inspire the people to give more and to give more freely.

If you run into police, show them the simple love of Jesus and that you have nothing to hide. Give them the lit and explane[sic] to them with enthusiasm and conviction what you are doing. This will lessen any fears or doubts they might have and often will result in a good donation.

The more God can break you, the more He can use you — burn out with a broken heart.

If you take a minute to speak in tongues, it'll lift your spirit.

You should enjoy litnessing as much as love-making.

COG members who excel in litnessing are referred to as "shiners," as opposed to "shamers" who fail to measure up to expectations. Jan's list of practical tips for more successful litnessing makes reference to a female member of the COG, Beraja, who is identified as "the shiner for the Northeast Region." Her record "Big Total" for thirty-six hours is listed as 6,832 pieces of literature. The commendation continues,

At times she has averaged 225 pieces per hour. How does she do it? No, she doesn't have wings. No, she isn't faster than the speed of light. No, she can't leap tall buildings in a single bound! How? She *burns free!* And hits the gas burners, the *cars!* Yes, she car litnesses — and this is another special car-litnessing-tip-section done by her for you. And if you car litness, please be extra prayerful and careful.

Some of Beraja's car litnessing tips include —

It's not good to wait; pick a corner where cars keep you busy all the time.

It's good to have a short green and a *long red.*

We get dirty faster in doing cars, but it's worth it. But it's not as dirty as working in cement companies or mines.

I keep saying to myself, "Beraja, you have to reflect the Kingdom of God, so they will read that precious letter and it will bring them life."

I'm sure it's possible to hit 12,000 a week. I know it. I have to die more to myself and put more hours in.

I found a good way to ask for donations. "We help young kids to get out of drugs; can you help us?" (Or can you give a quarter, a dollar, five dollars, fifty dollars?) Even if they said no at first, most of the old people melt and pull [sic] their dollars.

Interestingly, Jan states that money matters were not discussed with members of the "Family" unless it was in the context of a colony meeting and the discussion concerned such things as how much the rent was, how much was being taken in, and how much was needed.

Jan also observed that the leaders appeared to live better than the rank-and-file members. "I remember one time seeing one of the leaders wearing a brand new pair of pants and a brand new shirt. He was really dressed nice. That blew my mind, because I always had to go through a box of other people's old clothes that they had discarded in order to get clothes for myself. So I said to one of my sisters, 'I wonder how come this guy always has new clothes?' I guess I said it to the wrong person, because she told one of the leaders what I had said. Then they took me aside and explained that this guy had to have nice clothes because he went and talked to big businessmen and tried to get donations.

"Leaders sometimes had beds and suitcases, expensive cameras, portable tape recorders. Concerning these possessions, the leaders would merely say, 'Oh, you'll get those things some day.' We were told that they had been donated to the group.

"None of the members of the group used drugs. Alcoholic beverages were permitted — in moderation. For instance, every once in a while we'd have a little bit of wine. If somebody offered us a beer, we could have a beer. But you weren't supposed to go out and get loaded. You were never supposed to buy booze. It was all God's money, not my money. (I never had a dime in my pocket, anyway.) Married couples were given five dollars a month to buy a couple bottles of wine so they could drink it and loosen up, as Mo said, before they had sex."

JAN DESCRIBES a typical day's activities in the COG: "We got up at 7:00 A.M., sometimes at 6:30. From 7:00 to 7:30 was wash-up time. From 7:30 to 8:00 we had prayer. From 8:00 to 8:30 was for memorization and review. We would study the Bible, memorize Scripture and Mo quotes. From 8:30 to 10:00 A.M. we read Mo letters. From 10:00 to 10:30 we had breakfast. From 10:30 to 11:00 we all got together and read some portion of the Bible. After that we did the dishes and cleaned up for an hour or so. By 12:00 P.M. we were to have all our literature ready in order to go out and hit the 'streets and sell Mo letters. We were expected to be back home by 6:00 P.M., and at 7:00 we'd eat dinner. At 8:00 we had a class, which would let out about 9:30, and then we'd have a snack. At 10:00 or 10:30 P.M., lights would be out and everybody had to go to bed. We followed that same fixed schedule every day, except one day a week when we would have a free day, during which we could do whatever we wanted to do. Very rarely, however, do I remember having a free day, because there was always something that had to be done. Even if you had a free day, you still were required to be with the Family, with a brother or sister.

"The young children in the group were treated very well. But they weren't really treated like children — they were treated more like little adults. They didn't seem to have the leeway that most little children have. If they were bad or if they did anything wrong, they were brought into the bathroom or taken outside and spanked. And they were spanked pretty hard — for any little offense at all they were spanked hard. Mo taught that parents should begin disciplining a child at the age of one-and-a-half or two years old. A child of two, just learning how to talk, knew more Bible verses and Mo quotes than anything else. It's kind of strange to hear a child that small crawling around reciting Bible verses. The kids all ate well and were given special attention because, as Mo put it, they represent our new blood, our 'new wine.'"

Whether young or old, all Children of God are familiar with Bible prophecy and Mo's prophecies. Jan was told that God's judgments were going to fall on the United States and that God "was going to wipe out America and kill all the evil people." The impending end of the world was a theme constantly referred to. "We were all going to head for the mountains, and God was going to send manna from the sky. We were His chosen ones, and we would someday rule over the earth for a thousand years, like it said in the Bible."

Professor Wallis describes the apocalyptic mission of the COG as follows:

> The Children of God have been mandated to gather out those who will commit themselves totally to Christ, forsake all, abandon the Whore of Babylon, the System, and suffer the coming persecution of the saints faithfully. Berg and his followers do not seek to gather just anyone into the fold. They employ the image of the "new wine." The older generation (and indeed anyone else who cannot accept the new wine of God's new revelations through Moses) are "old bottles" which would break under its impact. They seek only the "new bottles" who can take this new wine and these they expect to find among the young, and particularly the "disinherited" and "dropped-out" young. Rather than gathering all believers, COG seeks to draw together and train cadres capable to face the Great Confusion and the Tribulation, underground if necessary and worthy to be rulers in the post-Advent Kingdom. They believe that the message must be preached throughout the world to every nation before Christ's return (p. 13).

JANICE EVANS believes that she probably would not have left the Children of God on her own. "No amount of talking would have ever gotten me out of there, because I was like a horse with blinders on. I could only see one way. I was so brainwashed that even my father and my mother had no effect on me at all. I remember one time talking to my parents on the telephone, and they were both crying and everyone else in my family was crying, and I thought, *What are they so upset about?* I had no emotional feelings whatsoever towards them. I hardly knew who i was talking to.

"One day I was walking down the street in Los Angeles with a brother, and a car pulled up along the street containing my father and my sister. Both of them lived on the East Coast, and so I was very surprised to see them. We talked and shared a little bit. I went back to the colony and got permission to spend the day with them. Of course, a brother from the colony came with us. We went to the hotel and talked and went out to dinner and had a really nice time. My father asked me to come home and see my mother before I went to Venezuela. (All of the Children of God were leaving America, and within the next few days I was scheduled to be on a plane on my way to Venezuela.)

"On the way back to my father's hotel, we were talking about calling my mother and telling her that I would come home. It was ripping my heart out because, after seeing my father, I wanted to see my mother. The experience had renewed all the love that I had for them.

"When we got back to his hotel and were about to go inside, my father asked me to please call my mother and tell her that I'd be coming home. I told him, 'Just let me pray one more time and see if it's the Lord's will.' I asked if I could go into the car to pray. This I did, and then my father asked, 'Can I come in and talk to you for just a minute?' I said, 'Yes, of course.'

"As my father got in on the driver's side, someone else got in on the passenger side, and another man got into the back seat with me. I started screaming: 'Dad, what's happening? Dad, what's going on, are you ripping me off?' I was amazed that it was happening to me, because we had always been told about people being kidnaped, but I never believed it would happen to me. My companion from the COG was standing there: he wanted to help me so much, but he couldn't. I screamed and waved my arms and tried to stomp on the gas and attempted to jerk the steering wheel, but they held me down and tried to calm me. Immediately I saw that I had to be cool. I had to make believe that everything was all right, because if I was upset, it was not going to be easy to escape. I knew that I had to be real cool, play their game, or else I wouldn't get out.

"They took dozens of rights and dozens of lefts and lost me completely. I had no idea where I was. Finally they brought me to this big house, this really beautiful home. The house was totally systemite in my eyes. They brought me into the house and talked to me for a long time. I went through the process known as deprograming. They talked to me, got me angry, got me exhausted, got me to think.

"I'm so grateful to the people who helped me get out of the COG. I feel like my life is indebted to them because before that time, I really had no life. I was just a zombie, a robot, a Moses David robot.

"For a few days after I was deprogramed, I stayed in the same house. Other former cult members came and visited me. They helped me so much. I was really in a fog — I had no idea if I was coming or going. I didn't know what was right and what was wrong. I was just totally confused. And they came, and they helped me so much just by being there and reassuring me. Half the deprograming, I'd say now, wasn't what they said to me or how they talked to me, but it was the love that I felt around me. I didn't think that there was love outside of the Children of God any more. I thought that all systemite love was superficial, but I saw that these people really cared and wanted to help me."

Jan's parents really cared. As she puts it, "I think that I am one of the luckiest persons in the world, because I've got the most beautiful parents in the world."

◆ THREE ◆

The Alamo Christian Foundation

GREG WILSON graduated from UCLA in 1970, became a musician, traveled widely, and played music in a group for about three years. "During that time I began to go on a kind of spiritual search, and it took me through some pretty strange experiences. I dabbled in Eastern philosophies and religions, but nothing satisfied me to any real degree. I was restless and never really had a home during that period of time. I had no close friends except for the people I played music with in the group.

"One time in Monterey I had an experience in which God rattled my cage, and I started reading the Bible for the first time in my life. Something in it really spoke to me more than anything else I had ever read. I embarked on a search to find someone who could show me a way of living — the way I thought Christ was telling me to live in the Bible. I left the musical group, and my search was getting desperate. I saw imperfection in the lives of everyone I met who claimed to be a Christian. I thought Christ was saying that there was a way to be perfect, and I wasn't finding anybody who was living that kind of life.

"I ended up in Santa Monica and started drinking to console myself, to drown my sorrows, because I sensed no direction at all in my life. I remember one morning walking around aimlessly near the Santa Monica pier where I encountered some young people passing out gospel tracts. I took one of their tracts and was really turned off by it. I read it over, and it just seemed like trash to me. And yet I was curious about the young people who were so aggressively passing out the gospel tracts to anybody who would take them. Eventually a couple of them approached me and gave me a real hellfire and brimstone message that if I didn't get right with God, I would spend all eternity in hell. I remember their directness and the really powerful way they witnessed to me. They looked me in the eye and pulled out the heavy-duty fear Scriptures in the Bible. They had quite an impact on me, and then they told me that they had a service at a church in Saugus. They said that a bus would be leaving that evening for Saugus and that they would provide transportation back. About ten minutes later, as I was walking back to my house, I got witnessed to by several others in the group who gave me the same powerful, confident, bold treatment.

"Back at the house, I reread the tract I had been given and noticed that it was distributed by an organization called, The Tony and Susan Alamo Christian Foundation. I felt the tract, which contained Tony's life story, was absurd. Yet I was so down on the life I was leading that I thought to myself, *Gosh, what am I going to do tonight?* It was Friday night, and I probably would sit around and play some music with the guy I was staying with, and end up getting drunk and wake up the next morning with no better prospects in sight. So I concluded, *You've got nothing to lose — you'll even get a free dinner there.* I didn't have much money at the time, so even that was pretty appealing.

"I was really turned off to churches up to that point in my life, and I hadn't attended church in a long time. I was curious to see what all these young kids were so fired up about, and so I decided at five that afternoon that I would go and check out the place. While on my way to the appointed place, I was really taken aback when this red, white, and blue bus pulled up. It had the word HEAVEN written across the front of it and TONY AND SUSAN ALAMO CHRISTIAN FOUNDATION on the side. I boarded it. It seemed funny at the time that no one really talked to me. Some people were reading; few were talking to each other."

AFTER THE long trip to Saugus, the bus brought Greg to what looked like an old, converted restaurant. The first thing that struck him was that there was no nonsense going on: everyone seemed to have a sense of direction, and no one was sitting idle. Many people were sitting at tables reading their Bibles, and strange noises were coming from a nearby room. Greg later learned that this was the prayer room and that the people were speaking in tongues before the service started.

"When the service finally got started, it began with loud, gospel rock music. Being a musician, it really spoke to me. In fact, I can remember kind of thinking to myself at the time, *I wonder if the Lord is bringing me here because of my musical ability. Perhaps He still wants to use my musical talents, but He wants to use it now for His purposes instead of the way I had been using it in the past.*

"Following the music, a number of people went up to the front and gave their testimony. People told how they had been saved and brought to the house of the living God (the Alamo Foundation). At the end of the service, an altar call was given and they asked those who were unsaved to come forward and repeat the sinner's prayer. I remember feeling really convicted and really confused. One of the brothers came up to me and grabbed me by the wrist and said, 'Come on. You have to come up here and get saved. The Lord's calling you, and you'll never know if He will be calling you again. Right now is your time. Don't take a chance on God turning His back on you.' So I went up and fell on my knees and said a sinner's prayer of repentance.

"It was really an emotional experience. I can remember crying. I can remember a feeling of great relief, a feeling of catharsis. When I stood up, a group of three or four brothers was standing around me and one of them said: 'It's really wonderful now that you're saved, but that's not enough. Now that you're saved, God requires of you that you get baptized in the Holy Spirit.' We all went into the prayer room. . . .

"I sat down on a sofa, and about four or five of the brothers formed a half-circle around me, and we began to chant, 'Praise you, thank you, Jesus; praise you, Jesus; thank you, Jesus' over and over again. We did this for so long that I lost all track of time. I began to hallucinate; I didn't know where I was. Everyone was chanting in unison, and in a kind of rhythmic monotonous tone. Pretty soon I knew that what was coming out of my mouth was not 'Thank you, Jesus; praise you, Jesus.' My tongue was thick and my mouth became dry, and at some point in time everybody thought I was speaking in other tongues. They were in a frenzy, praising God and shouting, 'Hallelujah!' I really didn't know what was happening. I was in a different state of mind than I had ever experienced before, and I certainly had had no prior exposure to what was called the baptism of the Holy Ghost.

"After we left the prayer room, there was never a moment when I was all by myself. There were at least three or four brothers around me all the time, asking me questions, telling me certain things, quoting Scripture, and saying, 'Now that God has saved you, and He has brought you into His house, He wants you to stay here. This is where He has called you in these end times.' When we sat down to dinner, the pressure was being put on me to make a clear decision as to whether I wanted to stay and walk with God or whether I wanted to turn my back on Him by leaving. I was told that since He had saved me from the horrible pit that I had been in, if I were to go back into the world I would run the risk of being turned over to a reprobate mind or turning into a homosexual or becoming insane. The group pressure was powerful. When one of them was at a loss for words, there was another ready with some kind of a Scripture, like, 'Abide in the calling wherein ye are called.' That verse was used to impress upon me the fact that God had called me to Foundation. That was where I was supposed to live, now that I was saved, and I was not supposed to go back into the world."

FOR TWO months prior to this experience, Greg had been searching for God. He had wanted to give his life to God. "I had given up my whole life of music, the group, playing clubs, making records. I was sincere in my desire to really want to live a life that was right, and to live a Christian life. So I said to myself, *Well, if this is true, if this is really where I have been called, sure, I want to live this new life.* I remembered that my car and all the rest of my belongings were still in Santa Monica. So I told them that I was going to go to Santa Monica and get my car and my clothes and go down to Mission Viejo and see my parents and tell them what I'd decided to do. Then I would come back to the Foundation and move in.''

But Greg's new friends rebuffed the idea: ''What makes you think you are strong enough now to go back out there alone and be able to withstand the devil? He's really going to come at you now that you're saved. What makes you think that you're strong enough to withstand him out there?''

Greg reports, ''I was also told that my parents would now be my worst enemies. They quoted Scripture verses about the division between father and son and mother and daughter. I stayed up that first night arguing with several of the brothers, until I finally collapsed out of exhaustion at two or three o'clock in the morning. I kept telling them, 'I'm not sixteen years old! All I want to do is go and pick up my car and my things, say hi to my parents and then I'll be right back here.' But they would keep quoting Scripture in response to everything I said: 'Look, this is the Word of God. You're not going to turn your back on God's Word, are you?'

''When I woke up the next morning, there were two or three brothers praying nearby with their Bibles open. I didn't feel like arguing any longer, so I finally agreed to allow three members of the Foundation to go with me to Santa Monica to pick up my car and my personal belongings. I told my former roommate that I had gotten saved and that I was moving into the Alamo Foundation. We returned to Saugus (without visiting my parents) and I still had a lot of doubts about my decision. I even remember thinking, 'Maybe I've been brought up here to shine some light into this weird place.' My doubts remained during the first week at the Foundation, but I was determined to see this thing through and to discover if God had really called me to this particular place, for whatever reason. I definitely wanted to do whatever He wanted me to do.''

At the Foundation, new converts are called ''baby Christians'' and are placed under the constant, watchful eyes of ''older brothers and sisters in the Lord.'' From these ''older Christians'' the new members learned that they must be ''100 percent for God'' and that if they leave the Foundation, they will lose their salvation. To follow God and be His disciples, the new recruits are warned that they must forsake mother and father because "Jesus demands *all* — anything less is not enough."

Greg soon discovered that his parents were lumped with Satan. "They really kept pounding this thing about my parents: 'Now watch out, because your parents are going to come here and they're going to try to get you out of here. That's how the devil is going to attack you. We've seen it time and time again. That's how the devil really comes at young Christians.' I couldn't picture my parents ever making a demand on me like that. But sure enough, about a week after I had been up there, my parents came to visit me after learning from my sister where I was.

"After my parents arrived, I wasn't allowed to be alone with them. We were told that you were never allowed to be alone because that was unscriptural. Even Christ sent His disciples out in two's; He never allowed them to go out one by one, because the devil could pick them off if they were alone. I never really talked to my parents that night. Any questions they asked were fielded by one of the older brothers. . . .

"When they were talking to my parents, an incredible feeling was going through me: 'They're right. These people are absolutely right. I can see that my parents *are* trying to get me out of here. The devil is using my parents. I can really see it. It happened just like they said. They had been saying it this whole week and here it is.' My parents were astonished. I remember my father saying, 'You mean to tell me, you can't even come out with us and go have a cup of coffee with us down at Newhall? What is this?' And I was thinking to myself, *Wow, they really are trying to get me out of here.* That night was really the clincher for me. I really bought the whole program after that."

TONY AND Susan Alamo began preaching to the hippies on the Hollywood Boulevard in the late sixties. The details of their lives up to then are hazy. Susan claims to have had a dramatic Christian experience as a young child. Later she left a brief career in show business to return to full-time evangelism. She met Tony at a Bible class she was teaching, and they were soon married. Tony was raised in a Jewish home and later emerged, according to his own claim, a successful Hollywood PR man and record promoter.

The Alamos assert that the Jesus movement began in Hollywood when they started handing out tracts and witnessing to youthful hippies and drug addicts. In 1970 the Alamos moved to the outskirts of Saugus, California, where they purchased a rambling old restaurant in Mint Canyon. Soon thereafter they acquired nearby acreage for dormitories. In the early days, the finances apparently were derived primarily from donations and a few small, local Foundation-operated businesses, including a gas station. Discarded food from bakeries and supermarkets provided the mainstay for meals.

The organization quickly grew to the point where hundreds of young converts crowded the nightly revival meetings and the overflowing dormitories. The Alamos' obvious success was also evidenced by a Cadillac Fleetwood with personalized license plates and a large house, situated on five prime acres and allegedly built with the "donated" labor of the Foundation faithful. An architectural student who had dropped out of college to join the Foundation assisted with the plans and supervised most of the construction. An ex-member of the Foundation reported that he had worked on the house twenty hours a day for over a month.

In 1975 the Alamo enterprise was expanded to include an additional church and several small businesses in the tiny town of Dyer, Arkansas. It was rumored that Tony and Susan had left California because of legal problems. This was denied by Tony, who claimed that the move had been made because of his wife's deteriorating health. He said she was suffering from terminal cancer. The day-to-day operation of the Saugus facility has been left to trusted lieutenants and spiritual "overseers." Foundation members are told to "contend" for Susie's healing. She is on a special diet and has reportedly lived seven years beyond her doctors' prediction. As one member put it, "The Lord has kept her. We are claiming her healing in the name of Jesus. Satan hates her and wishes to destroy her. She's so close to God; she's a powerhouse for Jesus. We're praying for Susie and the Lord to bind the devil."

It didn't take long for Greg to discover that the brothers and sisters at the Alamo Foundation pray a great deal. "We were taught to always be in prayer because the Bible teaches you to pray in season and out of season. We were taught to wake up in the morning praising and thanking God. One of the older brothers had awakened me in the morning by shaking me and saying, 'Wake up, Greg; praise you, Jesus; thank you, Jesus.' You are required to be on your feet within one minute praising and thanking God. You would have to wake up saying aloud, 'Praise you, Jesus; thank you, Jesus.' You were taught to repeat that phrase either in your mind or out loud as much as you could all day long.

"I soon became a real zealot. I was praying for four or five hours a day and would read the Bible every chance I had. I began to move out of the 'baby Christian' stage and was given new responsibilities and duties. Still, I was never allowed to be alone. There were times when I had doubts. But whenever that happened and I began to ask questions, there would be four or five brothers right there on the spot. They would literally form a circle around you, and if one of them couldn't answer a question, certainly one of the others would. They would go through their Bibles and point out how I was wrong. 'You're going against God. You are really running the risk of being turned over to a reprobate mind.' I conformed and eventually worked my way up to being an overseer.

"During the last five months of my stay at the Foundation, I was shipped out weekly to the fields around Bakersfield to do farm labor work. The experience of working in the fields was incredible. The living conditions were horrible. At one point, for about a month and a half we lived in a house near Shafter while we were picking fruit. It was a four-room house and anywhere from eighty to one hundred of us lived there all week long. It had hardwood floors, wooden walls with no insulation, no furniture, and no heating. This was in November and December in the San Joaquin Valley, where it gets cold and damp....

"I can remember mice running over the floor and through the sleeping bags at night. I can remember sometimes feeling so pent up inside because when you're crowded like that, the pressure inside you builds up so that you feel like screaming at the top of your lungs.

"We were led to believe that all these discomforts were the trials and tribulations that we were going through to make us strong. This was the Lord's chastening to get His people ready for the horrible time of tribulation that was coming upon the earth. We were told, 'Count it all joy — crucify the flesh.' That's when you started praying, 'Thank you, Jesus; praise you, Jesus. Oh, Lord, help me to be thankful for this.' And meanwhile you were just going out of your mind. It was just horrible.

"There were a lot of health problems at the Foundation in Saugus. People's teeth were literally rotting and falling out in some cases. We had a lot of intestinal troubles, probably because of the way in which the food was obtained. The Alamo Foundation had various grocery stores in the L.A. area from which they would get old produce and old dairy products, dated food that had been removed from the grocery shelves and disposed of. We'd spend hours in the kitchen trying to sort out the good from the bad, and a lot of the bad got through. Everyone experienced what we affectionately termed the RGB's (rot gut burps). Now I had lived in some pretty raunchy conditions while I traveled around as a musician, and never had I experienced anything like that. . . .

"When we were doing farm labor work, we worked just like madmen. The braceros were amazed and used to gawk at us while we were working. We wouldn't even stop for a drink of water because we were led to believe that every orange that we picked was another soul that was going to be saved through our ministry. That's why I lost so much weight (forty pounds), and all the other people did too. We worked like crazy and turned over all of our money to the Foundation. During the last three or four months I was there, I never even saw a paycheck. And we made good money. I guess I made about $3,000 while working on the farms. We just turned it all over to the older brothers, and they in turn handed it over to Tony and Susan, I guess. There were hundreds of us working in the fields at that time, so they were taking in an awful lot of money. I can remember making well over $200 picking olives. The girls worked too, pruning grapevines, tying vines. There were always jobs to do."

FEW PEOPLE, inside or outside the Foundation, have specific information regarding its finances. The Alamos are very guarded in their statements regarding membership and income. The Alamos stress that much of the income for their tax-exempt organization is derived from donations. A weekly thirty-minute telecast aired by a number of independent TV stations has been another source of funds in recent years.

Tony and Susan apparently do not attempt to hide their personal prosperity. Greg was very much aware of their affluent life style. "Every time I saw them, they were dressed to the teeth. Tony would have a leather jacket on, slacks and real expensive shoes and jewelry. Susan dresses like the queen — super-expensive dresses. Never did I see her without her hair completely done up. They drive brand new Lincoln Continentals. Not a new Chevrolet, or a new Ford — black Lincoln Continentals with ALAMO on the license plates."

Tony and Susan's followers don't seem to mind the dual standard of living — one for the leaders, and an entirely different one for the rank-and-file. Tony and Susan are their "spiritual parents," their "pastors in the Lord," who are due "double honor." Greg came to believe that the Alamos' affluence was God's reward for their long years of devoted service. "They had been in it for so long that they were not in danger of losing their souls to the temptations of the flesh. God was giving them their just deserts for hanging in there that long. We were told that if we were faithful, God would give us these things too. But for the present, we had to crucify our flesh."

Crucifying the flesh meant, among other things, a weekly shower after many days of arduous agricultural labor in the fields. "Once a week we would be brought back to Saugus for our Sunday service. If we were lucky, it was our one chance during the week to get a shower. We had one shower for about 200 males at what was called Saugus No. 2 on Sierra Highway. To get a shower you would wake yourself up at three or four o'clock in the morning. There was only cold water, never hot water.... To make matters worse, the toilets were always backed up. There were two toilets for those two hundred males: one sink, two toilets, and one shower.

"We would return from Bakersfield about ten at night and

would be told that we would be leaving at eight the next morning to go up to Tony and Susan's house to put on our suits for the TV show. After a night in the showers, we would board the buses at 8:00 A.M. and leave for Tony and Susan's house, where our suits were stored. We would again have to wait in a long line for the clothes to be distributed. We would stand outside in the cold December morning, some of us with wet heads from the showers, waiting until our names were called. You would grab your suit and then would have to wait in another long line to get into a separate building where we would change our clothes. That room only held about twelve people and there was no room to move around. Finally, after changing, we would go back and board the bus. The whole procedure would take perhaps an hour and a half. We felt like cattle — herded into one line and then herded into another line only to be crowded onto the buses for the ride to Hollywood where the TV shows were filmed. Four shows would be filmed in a single taping session. We would be there for as long as six hours, standing up the whole time. One time when we were singing, one of the brothers next to me just collapsed, passed out. A couple of us just held onto him because it was near the end of one of the singing segments and we didn't want to blow the tape. He had collapsed from exhaustion and the stifling heat of the studio. Before we started taping the next show he managed to go and sit down by himself some place.

"We were always told to smile a certain way during the TV show. Susan would come in beforehand and tell us what was expected. We had to be presentable — smiling, looking like all-American boys and girls, very rigid and stiff. We had to be a witness."

Some of the brothers and sisters who were featured on the TV programs comprised the inner circle or elite of the Alamo Foundation. There were about twenty-five or thirty guys and girls at the top. They would ride around in the Continentals and Cadillacs and were allowed to live near Tony's house. They sang on the TV shows and got to sit in the sound studio when the records were cut. Everyone else had to stand up on the hard wooden floors.

"It was just like a two-class system," Greg says. "There was a real dividing line. The older brothers at the top and those aspiring to be leaders lived better and even looked a little different from the rest of us.

"Tony and Susan are totally removed from the rank-and-file membership. I never once talked to Susan, not even on the telephone. She never said hi to me; she never knew my name, I am sure. I only talked to Tony one time while I was there, and that was just a couple of days after I had arrived. He called me on the phone and asked me if I wanted to stay at the Foundation. He listed the rules, the dos and don'ts, and asked if I was willing to abide by those rules. He asked if I was willing to turn over my possessions to the group, and then he assigned me my older Christian. That's the only time I ever talked to Tony."

WHEN TONY and Susan appear before a church service at the Foundation, their reception is similar to that accorded a movie star, a leading political figure, or latter-day apostle. Prior to their entrance, there would be a sense of anticipation in the air. Some of the young people would whisper inquiringly, "Is Sue coming? Are they coming?" Frequently a phone call would be received informing the audience that the pastors would be forty-five minutes late.

Susan, a platinum blonde probably in her late fifties, is clearly the preacher of the pair. Her sermons are a strange admixture of the wrath of God and the rhetoric of Susan Alamo. She lashes out at the lukewarm churches and the "God is Love heresy" that they preach. All the churches are dead, but the Foundation is at the forefront of a revival that is sweeping America and will sweep the world. America is falling fast into the hands of communism. These are the last days, and Satan is attacking hard because he knows his time is short.

Susan Alamo has been elevated by her ardent admirers to a position approaching sainthood. As one ex-member put it, "Some of the kids there are former drug addicts. Now they are addicted to Sue." Greg states that members were told that Susan was healed of cancer several times and that it was only through the prayers of the people in the Foundation that she was kept alive. "You are constantly taught that the most important prayer you can pray is to pray for Susie's healing. If you really want to chalk up points from God, you've got to pray for Susie to be healed. Every word that comes out of her mouth is 'directly from the throne of the living God.' It's like God speaking through her. What she says is almost equivalent to the Scriptures. In fact, they would play tapes of her messages while we were eating lunch out in the fields. It was considered similar to reading the Book of John or First Peter."

On the telecasts, Tony sings and Susan preaches. In a rambling and ungrammatical fashion, she reiterates the dramatic evidence of their successful ministry to the young people that no one else cared for, especially the churches. She reminds her audience, however, that their bold efforts for God and country meet increasing opposition. Satan is on the offensive and "trouble makers" are on the loose. Susan assures the TV audience that the "wild stories" about happenings at the Foundation are "filthy lies" spread by "outside agitators." As a result of their persecution, Tony and Susan cast themselves in the role of fighters for religious freedom. They predict a day when they will be placed behind prison bars for holding fast to the truth.

IF IN FACT Tony and Sue ever do find themselves in jail, it will not be the result of their preaching the gospel. Accusations of alleged mind control, deplorable living conditions, beatings, and slave labor have been leveled by parents, relatives, and other concerned citizens. In August 1974, the State Senate Select Committee on Children and Youth held a hearing on the activities of various cult groups active in California, including the Alamo Foundation. Testimony was given regarding the squalid living conditions at Saugus, the lack of proper medical attention, and the spiritual-psychological manipulation of the youthful converts. Susan Alamo's own daughter testified that she left the group after she could no longer countenance what was going on. She told about young people being told to get down on their knees and accept Jesus Christ, when in fact they were "accepting my mother." She described people living in converted "chicken coops" with no heat, no lights, and no toilet. One day she simply told her mother, "I'm leaving! I want out; I can't take it any more. I can't look at little children being treated like little dogs." The daughter claims that her life has been threatened.

Greg encountered a rigid legalism at the Foundation. Members were encouraged to observe one another's behavior, and an elaborate reporting system was devised for those who strayed from the carefully demarcated path. Following is an example of a written report critical of one young woman's behavior:

Sisters' Report
Judy Brown

Judy Brown was sitting outside of the Saugus #8 kitchen by herself at 5:30 a.m. waiting for the van to take the Ontario sisters to work.

I told Judy B. twice to come inside and that it was a rule not to be outside the apartments at night.

Judy B. did not receive my advice either time but told me just to write her on report.

Confirmed by: Reported by:

[date]   Witnessed by:

When he left the Foundation, Greg brought with him a list of some seventy-one "group offenses" which Foundation members were taught to avoid. Here is a representative sampling from that list of offenses:

Entering the kitchen without permission except during services.

Slide furniture over any floor.

Talking too loud after evening service in front of church.

To interrupt a group unnecessarily while they are reading.

For driver to refuse to drive without good excuse.

Bring vehicle back with less than ¼ tank of gas.

Let vehicle run out of gas.

Not get stamps when buying gas at other than Foundation gas station.

Step on flowers.

Hang clothes to dry on fireplace screens.

Enter tract room without permission.

Not be back at witnessing vehicle at designated time.

Not put yourself on wake-up 25 minutes before your baby Christian.

To leave a baby Christian unattended or not assign him to baby Christian watcher.

Late for choir or band practice without good excuse.

To be motionless one minute or more while in prayer room.

Not get up in five minutes.

One late wake-up past ten minutes or three late wake-ups under ten minutes.

Nod during services.

Not turn in donation cards filled out properly.

Damage tracts.

For the new recruits at the Foundation, there were three so-called "baby Christian offenses."

1. Refuse night watch without good excuse.
2. Sleep during service, night watch or prayer hour.
3. Pick up cigarette butts off street while witnessing.

Committing a group offense resulted in being placed in a special group for a period of time ranging from a couple of days, to a week, or even a month. "Being in a group is like K.P. in the army. You spent your whole time every day all day in the kitchen washing dishes, pulling K.P., sorting out all that horrible, rotten food and produce. The rest of the time you were with one of the older brothers praying and reading the Bible in a group. You get very little sleep while you are part of a group."

Relationships between the sexes are also carefully governed at the Foundation. Leaders reject the label "Christian commune" because of possible sexual connotations associated with that term.

Segregation along sexual lines at the Foundation is total. Men and women live not only separately but far apart. Contact of any sort is strictly forbidden. Lewd clothing, a judgment made by Tony's trained eye, is outlawed, as is talking to members of the opposite sex except at meal time, and then only with a female-male ratio of three to one. Marriage is permitted with the approval of the Alamos, but

only after a total separation of 90 days reserved for praying
and fasting (*The Jesus People*, p. 63).

DESPITE THEIR incredible legalism, members of the Foundation believe it is possible to live without sin. Greg notes, "They
say that you *can* sin, that there are people who *maybe* sin once
in a while at the Alamo Foundation. But that's where grace
comes in. God will cover those little teeny bloopers that you
make — their term is 'blowing it.' But God has given you the
power of the Holy Ghost, and if you are in the Spirit, He isn't
going to allow you to sin. If you do sin, you are out of the Spirit
and you better really watch out: the devil might gobble you up
and you might end up in an institution someplace."

Anyone not part of the Foundation is considered to be
outside the body of Christ. "That even includes other Christians. They really believe that they are the only group which
has the truth. All other so-called 'Christian' groups have either
backslidden or are deceived or are lukewarm. They will admit
that there *might* be some Christians out in the world that are
really walking with God, but they haven't met them yet. For the
most part, all of the people that are not in the Alamo Foundation are possessed of the devil. They really believe that a large
proportion are reprobates who literally have deliberately
turned their backs on God. There is no hope for them. They are
pawns of the devil." This attitude, it might be added, does not
come across on the Alamo TV program. Born-again viewers are
encouraged to write and give financial support to "this work of
God."

Greg recalls one of those rare occasions when he talked
with a couple of older brothers who had been allowed to go out
as a witnessing team to the Pacific Northwest. "They came back
with these stories saying that no one anywhere was really
walking with God like the Alamo Foundation. We were the
only ones. In fact, we were Joel's army — the army that was
prophesied in the Old Testament to be raised up in the end
times. We were told to be real warriors because God was going
to use us to save the world. They actually believe that at some
point in time God is going to call a lot of them to go to Jerusalem
in order to witness to the Jews and save Israel.

"I recall Tony saying that we would become God's strong

'bulldogs.' I also remember Tony praying: 'Make us mudpie puppets for God.' 'Make us robots for God.' There were times when we prayed like robots. I remember praying one time for hours — all night long in fact — against the devil coming against us in the form of Baxter Ward [L.A. political figure]. Ward was investigating our church, and he represented the devil himself. We were screaming up and down the church for one whole night, praying against the devil, Baxter Ward."

Not everyone who came to the Foundation stayed. Greg observed a rather large turnover of people.

He recalls a particular incident that took place on a witnessing trip to Santa Monica. "One member of the witnessing team was a Mexican-American who happened to be an epileptic. He had stopped taking his medication, Bilantin, when he joined the Foundation because 'epilepsy was just an affliction of the devil.' And now that he was saved, God had healed him and he didn't need it any more. Well, he had a grand mal seizure on the bus on the freeway and had to be held down. He was thrashing all about and making a bloody mess. It was horrible! One guy finally got his belt off and put it in his mouth. Everybody was praying out loud, 'The blood of Jesus against you, Satan!' We believed that Satan was literally trying to get into his body.

"Finally things kind of subsided, but the man still had a dazed look. His eyes were big and dilated. We finally arrived in Santa Monica and were all told to get off the bus and go out and witness. Two of the older brothers were going to stay with the epileptic. So we took our pamphlets and went out to witness. When we returned, the story we were told was: 'Well, the devil just got into him and he refused to fight. He stopped praying, and the devil got ahold of him and he's gone.'

"To this day I don't know what actually happened to him. That's the only story we ever got. I don't know if they got rid of him or if he walked off by himself. There were other instances when individuals would be with you and then, during the night, they would simply vanish. The overseers would say, 'Well, he's left' or 'He's gone' or 'The devil got him.' I'm sure most just got up and left on their own. But I also think that some of them were dumped off in the desert at night. I know of one such case for sure. How many others suffered a similar fate? How do you check on things like that?

"Some people would be embarrassed to even admit that they were part of a group like that. People who end up getting involved in a cult experience like this often find it difficult to talk about. Lots of times when I started to talk about it to people, I would just say, 'Forget it.' They think I'm totally crazy or some kind of lunatic. . . . I have had a hard time myself accepting the fact that it actually happened to me."

WHAT ABOUT the young people who give such glowing public testimonies — what accounts for their apparent satisfaction? Greg believes their behavior can best be explained in the context of strong group pressures and a kind of mind control. "Every day is such an ordeal — the work, the prayer, the reading. You just chomp at the bit for any opportunity to be the center of anything. The minute you get any opportunity to speak, why, that is your ultimate! To get up and give a testimony in church, to go down and witness on the street — you live for these moments. Just to be able to shine your light, to be able to have God use you. All that pent-up energy comes out and you feel a definite glow, because the rest of your life is so miserable — you are crucifying your flesh, shutting off your mind. The minute you get a chance to put that six hours of reading into practice, you say, 'Oh, thank God!' Also, the group peer pressure in that kind of a situation is really powerful. You know that everyone around you is expecting you to perform. God is expecting you to perform.

"Another scriptural admonition we received in this regard was to 'be deceivers yet true.' This means that if you are hurting inside, for example, when witnessing, that's the devil coming at you. God asks you to ignore the devil and to be a deceiver. Even though you hurt inside, God's telling you to be true because you are speaking the word of truth."

Another form of deception is used when visitors arrive at the Saugus property. According to Greg, visitors are shown only what the leaders want them to see. They are permitted to view the showcase living quarters of the Foundation upper crust. Rank-and-file members rarely saw the inside of those apartments, as Greg relates. "There was one really nice house where about six of the older brothers lived. I was allowed to go there and to take a shower one time, and I mean it was a big deal. I walked in and it was a real house! Real shower! We were told that maybe sometime in the future, God had this in store for each and every one of us. This was the kind of thing that the visiting journalists are shown. They don't see Saugus No. 2. They don't get to see that house in Shafter. They are shown the sanctuary and they are served a meal. What they don't know is that we always sorted out separate food for Susan. There was also a separate pile for certain of the older brothers and sisters. They actually had their names on the piles of food. The remainder went to the rest of the people."

Although there are conflicting opinions on the topic, Greg strongly feels that the diet at the Foundation was inadequate and not well-balanced. Some of the members gained weight; others, like Greg, lost a lot. "In my opinion, all of us were in a state of semi-malnutrition. We ate a lot of pasta and white bread. Very rarely did we receive meat. Twice while I was there they killed two cows. When distributed among four or five hundred people, however, that amounted to just a little chunk of beef for each of us. We got a little piece of roast on our plates and thought, *Wow! The Lord is sending manna down from heaven.*"

Greg also reports that they were encouraged, on the authority of Scripture, to practice fasting. "I fasted one time for five days. It was in the winter. We were snowed in. It was a really good way to crucify my flesh. You go into a state where you feel like you don't even need food any more. After about the second day, you're not even hungry any more. You experienced a feeling of euphoria, a kind of floating around. Then you are really in a state of suggestibility."

Greg feels that the group's constant chanting or praying was actually a form of auto-suggestion. "I got real good at it. We were taught that our mind was of the devil, so that any time any kind of thought came in which conflicted with the group mind or contradicted the group mind, we were led to believe that the devil himself was putting words in our mind. The only way you could counteract that was to recognize the devil, and he would flee. The way you made him flee was through prayer. You would say, 'Thank you, Jesus; praise you, Jesus,' and just get those thoughts out of there. If you do that long enough, it becomes a form of self-hypnosis. When you're chanting that way, you get that 'thousand-mile stare.' I think that is the real key to the kind of manipulation, the kind of power and control they have over people at the Foundation."

Besides inadequate food, Greg discusses another form of sensory deprivation: lack of sleep. "I thought I was really lucky if I could get four or five hours of sleep a night. We were awakened at all hours of the night. You never knew when you were going to be awakened: you might have to pray for something. For example, we were told, 'Susie's ill.' Everybody would get up and pray. They also had what were called 'night watchmen' at all of the buildings, posting watch all night long, at two-hour intervals. So you might be awakened to take the watch for two hours.

"If you were not awake within a minute and on your feet praising and thanking the Lord, you were reported. . . .

"I never experienced the feeling of rest or peace, because you didn't know when you might be awakened. You were in a constant state of anxiety, because it was possible that you might be awakened again in two or three hours to go pray for an hour.

"Likewise, our day-to-day activities might change without prior warning. For example, we might be told that we had to start picking apples tomorrow morning. 'Get up, Greg — praise you, Jesus; thank you, Jesus; praise you, Jesus — we've got to go! The bus is going to leave in fifteen minutes. Get your stuff. We're going down to Tehachapi. We're going to be picking apples this week.' You never knew where you would be going, what you would be doing. Also, if you did have a little spare time, you were told to 'redeem the time.' If you really wanted points with God, if you really wanted to be a bulldog for God, you had to redeem the time. That meant you had better start reading, or you had better start praying."

None of the faithful knew what Tony and Susan were doing with their spare time. They were securely ensconced in their beautiful home high on a hill. "It's like a fortress. Next to the mansion is a two-story structure called 'The Windmill,' where several of the older brothers live. A watch is on duty constantly. The phone connects Tony's house to the Windmill. All the phones go through that line. The road to their house is constantly guarded. Members are not even allowed to walk past the front of their house. For example, if you are going there to put on your suit for the TV show, it would be a group offense just to walk in front of the house. You had to walk all the way down the side and around the back. You felt like a second-class citizen."

GREG'S PARENTS made one more trip to the Foundation after their initial visit. They returned with what Greg termed a "contrite spirit." There would be no more "hot-headed stuff" — they were going to be nice and sit through the service and see their son. But when they left, they said, "That's not even our son. We can't even talk to him. It's like a total vacuum." Mr. and Mrs. Wilson said they would never go back: they felt as if they had lost a son.

About a month or two after that last visit, Greg's parents were watching a talk show on TV which featured Ted Patrick talking about deprograming and his experiences with the various cults. As they listened to Patrick talk about brainwashing, they concluded, "That's what's happened to Greg. Everything he is saying sounds just like Greg's situation. We've got to get in touch with this guy. He's the first person we have heard who has said anything that sheds light on what's happened to Greg."

Eventually Greg's parents made contact with Ted Patrick. The first thing he told them was, "You have to get him out of there." How? "You've got to kidnap him." After discussing the pros and cons, Greg's parents decided they would do it.

Greg relates the story in retrospect: "They planned it thoroughly with the help of some relatives of mine who were big guys, fortunately. They even went up there and cased the grounds and found different roads they were going to use. They took two different cars in order to make a car switch. They had the whole thing really down.

"It was Sunday, and I was sitting in my chair waiting for the service to start, reading the Bible. One of the brothers came up to me and said, 'Your parents are here, Greg.' So I got up and met them just inside the front doors. While I was at the Foundation, I had been praying constantly for them. I wanted the Lord to bring them in out of darkness, release them from the bond of the devil. I wanted them to come to the Alamo Foundation, because Christ might be returning any day and I wanted my parents to be raptured along with me. When I saw them, I thought, 'God is answering my prayers. They've come up today, and I know they are going to see the light, finally. They're going to get saved today, and it's going to be wonderful!

"I heard my mom say something about my cousins being there with them. She said, 'They feel a little funny about coming in, because they haven't been invited. Maybe if you came out and invited them, they would come in and we could all sit through the service.' It was a group offense to go anywhere by yourself, and as a rule I would never have gone out that front door by myself. But that particular time I did.

"The timing was incredible. Tony and Susan were on their way to the church service with their entire band of six-to-eight bodyguards (Susan refers to them as 'her big boys'). You don't get near Tony without going through them. And they were all coming to the service.

"I went out through the front door of the church and walked to the car with my folks. I opened up the back door and reached in to shake hands with my cousin's husband. He grabbed me by the hand, and he yanked me inside the car while my dad pushed me from behind. I started pleading the blood of Jesus against them. 'Get thee hence, Satan!' They all looked like devils to me. I was fighting for my life. Then another relative leaped out of the bushes someplace and also jumped in the back seat with me. I was sandwiched between these two big brutes.

"My dad jumped into the passenger side on the front seat; my mom already had the engine going. We took off just as the brothers started to reach the car. By then, they were pouring out of the church. We tore off down the road, went about five hundred yards, and then pulled off the roadway on to a dirt area where the second car, which I recognized as my cousin's car, was waiting. They proceeded to drag me out of my dad's car and attempted to force me into the other car. I said, 'Man, you'll never get me into that car!' I fought. I broke the window of the second car. Finally I was pushed into the car, and we roared off in another direction in order to confuse anyone who might be following us.

"I was taken to a private home in the Los Angeles area, where I knew an attempt would be made to deprogram me. Everyone at the Foundation was warned about Ted Patrick. We knew that the spirit of antichrist was working in Patrick. If there was a devil walking the face of the earth today, it was Ted Patrick. We were told that he and his associates were going around capturing Christians and making them deny the Lord.

"I had been reading my King James Version of the Bible out loud during the whole trip from Saugus. I was reading in the Book of Hebrews when we turned the corner and passed a synagogue. I remember thinking, *Oh dear Lord, I'm going to be delivered up to a synagogue!* I'll never forget that feeling. When we arrived at the house I asked, 'Am I going to see Ted Patrick pretty soon?' This was to be my hour of temptation. Hallelujah! I was rejoicing because the Lord was finding me worthy to go through this. I kept saying, 'Lord, I won't deny you. I don't care if they poke my eyes out with hot sticks or if they light a fire under my feet. I am not going to give in.' And of course, I was chanting during the entire time. I was really in high gear: 'Praise you, Jesus; thank you, Jesus.'

"There were a number of people in that house that night, and I can't really remember what we were talking about. When you are in a state of chanting like that, your mind automatically screens out any contradictory or challenging input. Whenever a question arose that I construed as an accusation against Tony and Susan, I couldn't allow that to come into my mind because that was the devil. So I would shut the thought out and chant 'Thank you, Jesus; praise you, Jesus.' 'Deprograming' is really an attempt to ask probing questions, to find those challenging areas, and to make the person use his reasoning powers. So they challenged me on something, and I didn't want to use my reason, because to reason is to give the devil a chance. Your mind is the devil. You're not supposed to use your mind. The Scripture they quote in support of not using your reasoning is: 'Lean not unto your own understanding.' Instead of leaning on our own understanding, we were taught to stick to Scripture memorized from the King James Version, or to give an answer based on something you had heard Susan say. To do otherwise was to give the devil an open door.

"As the evening progressed, the pressure began to mount up. People were trying to talk to me, and I was saying, 'Praise you, Jesus; thank you, Jesus.' I wasn't going to allow the devil in. I kept it up until finally, out of sheer exhaustion, I passed out on the sofa. I never became violent. I had resigned myself to being there, because I believed that somehow God was going to deliver me. I knew I couldn't force my way out of the place — there were too many people, and besides, I am not basically a violent person anyway.

"I slept well that night and had some delicious food the next day. They continued to talk to me and to challenge my thinking. I felt like I was fighting a battle, and I tried to dig my meat hooks in harder and harder. I said to myself, Lord, I'm not going to do it. And then I went to bed and was allowed to get a good night's sleep for the first time in over half a year.

"The next day I remembered one of the questions my dad had asked the previous night right before I went to sleep. He said something to the effect that all of us were there to seek the truth and God says, 'Come, let us reason together.' I remember my dad saying, 'I'm your father. I love you. We all want to live according to the precepts of Christ. We need to go back to the Golden Rule and do unto others as we would have them do unto us. If you had the opportunity to have the power and the resources and the money that Tony and Susan have at their disposal, would you use that money to go out and buy two brand new Lincoln Continentals and a Cadillac limousine? Would you dress the way they dress? Would you spend the money to build a beautiful home high on a hill in Saugus? Or do you think you would use that money to really share with the brothers and sisters? Would you work together with them as a unit, or would you be removed from the actual body?' I had a hard time answering that question. I wanted to defend the Alamos. In fact, I think I did say, 'God has showered them now with blessings because they went without for so long.' I didn't want to admit that my dad was right.

"When I woke up in the morning, we had a good breakfast. We were sitting around talking when all of a sudden, just like that, I snapped out of it. It was just like turning on a light bulb. It was that quick. I just knew I was free! It was such a relief! I can remember hugging my mom. My chest was just heaving."

Today Greg attends an evangelical church and teaches public school in Southern California.

◆ FOUR ◆

The Love Family

DURING THE late summer of 1971 when the Jesus People revival was sweeping across the West Coast, Karen Taylor committed her life to Christ and went to live at a Christian ranch in California. One day she and a friend decided to hitch-hike up the coast to Canada; her friend, a Canadian citizen, was planning to visit an old boyfriend in Vancouver. When they reached the Canadian border, Karen decided to return to Seattle for lack of funds.

"I told my friend I would go back to Seattle and find a Christian house and wait for her. . . . I met some folks who said that they had stayed with the Love Family the previous night, and they found them to be real nice people. So I decided to look up the Love Family in the Queen Anne Hill district of Seattle.

"When I first got there, I was impressed with these people who said they believed in Jesus Christ and read the Bible. They really had class and did things nicely, not like most of the Jesus People I had met who were really corny. The Love Family did things in style, and they were really self-assured. About an hour after I got there, I felt that this was the place I was to be.

"When I walked into the house, there were about five or six people sitting around in the living room talking. One of the elders talked to me, and he was really nice, really friendly and polite. He talked to me about Jesus Christ and about being one family based on love. Their life seemed very ordered. . . .

"One of the elders encouraged me to read their charter, which was a statement of their beliefs. I looked at it, and it contained a lot of stuff from the New Testament, so I just figured it was a condensed version of the New Testament."

That document was actually the charter of the Church of Armageddon, the official name of the group she had stumbled upon. The charter states that the church is founded upon the revelation of Jesus Christ and welcomes "all people who sincerely desire to live the New Testament without hypocrisy." The document continues, "The Church of Armageddon was directed by God our father through the Lord Jesus Christ to fulfill the New Testament as revealed to Love Israel. . . ."

Love Israel is the founder and self-proclaimed leader of the Love Family. Formerly known as Paul Erdman, the one-time salesman arrived in Seattle in 1969 from California. Over a period of time he gathered around him a group of followers who believed that he is Christ's representative whose noble purpose it is to gather together God's true family. The charter quotes exclusively from the King James Version of the Bible and discloses that the name of the church was derived from the verse which reads, "He gathered them together into a place called in the Hebrew tongue Armageddon" (Rev. 16:16). The charter further describes the group thus:

> The Love Family is a real family, based on love and truth, based on God and Jesus Christ. The Love Family is the Church of Armageddon, the gathering of God's people, the eternal family of God. The Love Family is a home for everyone who loves.

"I stayed on for about three weeks and never heard from my Canadian friend," Karen relates. "Then I received an urgent telegram from my boyfriend asking me to call him. He hadn't heard from me, and he didn't know what was happening. I felt really bad about not having written to him, so I went back and stayed with him for about five weeks. After that I returned to Seattle with all of my belongings and moved in with the Love Family. I had also become pregnant during that five-week period."

At the time Karen joined the group, there were about sixty

people in the Love Family. They occupied seven houses, some of them old, some of them rented. Love Israel was the head of the entire Family, and each house was presided over by an elder. By 1976, they were occupying nine houses, only one of which was rented. In addition, the Church of Armageddon — whose membership had swelled to around two hundred — has a 160-acre ranch which it farms near Arlington, about forty miles north of Seattle. The group has also established branch colonies in Alaska and Hawaii.

For the first few days of her stay, Karen was essentially a visitor. There was no high-pressure attempt to get her to join. She was generally impressed with their life style, however, and after returning from her five-week visit with her boyfriend, she told them she would like to join the church. A waiting period of several weeks followed before she was baptized and formally admitted. The rite of baptism was a public ceremony that everyone in the church attended. Sometimes a neighbor's swimming pool would be used; in Karen's case, a bathtub sufficed. At that time she was also given a Bible name.

NAMES HOLD special significance in the Church of Armageddon. They teach that Israel is the name of God's people and that all true Christians are Israelites. The charter states, "The Kingdom of God is a state of love, a family that can never end, the Love Family. Our family surname is Israel. Our duty is to show mankind that Love Is Real."

The biblical names assigned at baptism are only temporary. Eventually each member is given a permanent holy name, a name of virtue, such as Meekness, Integrity, Happiness, Courage, and Patience. According to the charter, "our former names of the past were fictitious. Our real names are eternal gifts from God, and are the virtues of Christ." Once a person joins the Church of Armageddon, his previous name is obliterated.

Karen explains it this way: "If you were a member, at some point God would send down your real name which was the virtue that you represented. God would reveal that name to Love Israel: he would name us. Occasionally the names came through other people. They would say, for example, 'I know what that person's name is.' Sometimes Love would say, 'No, that's not it.'

"I received my virtue name about a year after I joined the group. Actually they knew my name before that point in time, but they wouldn't give it to me because I was too fat. Also, they weren't sure of me because I still had an attachment to Tom, my boyfriend. I had to really prove myself, prove that I was eternally a member of the Love Family and that I had no attachments in any other place."

Karen remembers well the day she received her virtue name. "Love invited me up to his room, which was very, very special. Few people ever went up there. He presented me with a little scroll that was inscribed, 'The Church of Armageddon,' along with my new name, the date, and a few other things which I no longer remember. He had it rolled up and tied with a ribbon and placed it on a velvet cushion.

"Not everyone received their name in that particular way. It was done differently to different people. The virtue names really had an affect on us. I was overwhelmed by my new name. People would try to identify with the virtue they represented. If your name was Patience, then you really tried to live up to that — you tried to be patient."

One thing the members of the Church of Armageddon did not identify with was their former family, their "natural" parents. "We were urged to cut off all communications with our parents. We were told that we shouldn't write to our parents, because when you are in Jesus Christ, you are starting a new life and the people of our past would hold us back. We had to give up all worldly ties, and our parents were tied with the world. We were separating ourselves from the world. New members are told, 'We are your only true family.' I referred to my biological parents as my 'worldly parents' or my 'natural parents,' but Love Israel didn't really like us to use the word parents at all. He wanted us to refer to them as simply 'Jane' and 'John.' They were viewed as people who just helped me along in the world. They were not my 'real' parents.

"The first thing we were told to do was to stop writing letters to our parents. As far as I was concerned, that was great, because my parents were always hassling me about writing. They wanted me to write every week, and I never wanted to write at all. I liked my parents, but I felt they were on my back, and I wanted to be free of them."

NOT ONLY did the Love Family change the names of individuals, but they also renamed the days of the week and the months of the year. The days of the week were named after the seven churches mentioned in the Book of Revelation: Ephesus, Smyrna, Laodicea, etc. Laodicea is the term for their Sabbath, observed on Saturday.

The months of the year were renamed after the twelve tribes of Israel. Each month was assigned thirty days, and the remaining five days were used for the celebration of the Passover. This made for some confusion: for example, a child born on July 22 would celebrate his birthday on the twentieth of Asher.

The time of day was determined on the pattern of New Testament times. The first hour of the day was six o'clock in the morning, the second hour was seven o'clock, and so forth. Also, the traditional manner of reckoning chronological age was modified by Love Israel according to his interpretation of the Bible. "We all got new ages: they were all sixty-six years older than our actual age," Karen notes.

The leaders of this particular group affirmed the need to break with the past by quoting out of context certain Bible verses containing the word now. "Now is the accepted time, behold now is the day of salvation" (2 Cor. 6:2); "Now is our salvation nearer than when we believed" (Rom. 13:11); (see also 1 Cor. 15:23; Eph. 2:13,14,19; 1 Cor. 12:18–20,24,25,27). "We were told that it was not good to talk about the past or the future. We were just to talk about the present. 'Now is the time.'"

Love Israel also influenced eating practices and the significance attached to food. The group supposedly observed the Old Testament rules concerning eating. "You weren't supposed to eat pork or shellfish and that kind of thing. Although if people donated those things, we would eat them. We would, but Love wouldn't. At times we got very little to eat. The amount of food available varied. . . . There was a lot of emphasis on not being fat. Love likes his women thin. But the men were not supposed to eat much either. But they were allowed to eat more than the women." Karen tells the story of a man who had fasted for three days, then at the dinner table downed twelve biscuits. He was asked to leave the group.

"Twice while I was a member of the group Love proclaimed a period of moderation. We were supposed to eat about a third of what we would normally eat. For example, for breakfast a person would have half a bowl of oatmeal and tea. At dinnertime you would be given a little scoop of rice and some vegetables and milk. That was it. Love felt that such occasions were spiritually necessary because we were getting too dependent on our food. He felt we should do without it for awhile.

"Sometimes selected individuals would be invited to Love's room as a special treat. One time I was invited to one of those intimate get-togethers, much to my great joy. We had salami and cheese and mayonaise and store-bought bread. Those things were really a treat.

"We baked most of our bread. We had a lot of grains, and we ground a lot of our own flour. We consumed a lot of tea but almost no coffee. Coffee was considered an addiction, although Love said we sometimes got addicted to tea, too. Wine was allowed, although Love had control over the wine. We made wine, and he supervised its distribution. All of the wine was drunk at his house during special occasions."

Other former members who joined the Love Family at a much later date report that large amounts of wine and beer are consumed on the Family's Sabbath. On that day, Love is said to don a brown velvet robe, and everyone gathers to greet their master. The celebration begins at high noon and includes singing and dancing.

Karen says they smoked marijuana and made marijuana cookies. Love provided the marijuana. "We also picked and ate mushrooms. We didn't try to identify whether they were good mushrooms or bad mushrooms. We only classified them according to whether or not they tasted good. We were taught that everything was from God and given to us to enjoy. We could take anything into our bodies and it wouldn't hurt us. All substances were taken in as a sacrament, as holy communion."

THE LOVE Family has made the headlines in Seattle several times because of their controversial "rite of breathing" involving the use of toluene, an industrial solvent. Inhaling toluene vapors was considered to be a religious ritual. "Everybody could do it. You had to do it at certain specified times, and you could never do it alone. You always did it in a group. It was very ritualized — we would sit around in a circle, and everybody would have a bag with a little toluene-soaked rag in it, and we would breathe it. It was something that was voluntary, but everybody loved it."

In January 1972, two young members of the cult were asphyxiated after inhaling toluene. They were discovered in the living room of one of their houses with plastic bags over their heads. The two men, Reverence and Solidity, were described as being disobedient in that they were in the room unsupervised. Another member of the Love Family reported to the press that Reverence had recently talked a great deal about death. "He had even prayed about it." The *Seattle Times* quoted a leader of the cult, Serious, as observing, "In a sense, God has freed his unhappy spirit from his body."

The leaders of the Church of Armageddon believed that the men had not really died and would revive in three days. They asked officials to delay an autopsy for three days "to allow for the possibility that God might restore their spirits to the same bodies, as He has resurrected many in the past."

The Love Family received a bad press as a result of the two deaths and later issued a statement clarifying their position.

> As Christians, who understand that nothing in God can really die, we are free to offer our bodies to God, in the hope that He can use us to help free all of mankind. From our experience, we cannot deny that certain organic chemical substances taken in the right environment and with the right motivation can help people.
>
> Our belief in Jesus Christ has freed us from the fears which, in the mind of the world, surround the use of these chemi-

cals. We have seen that we have eternal life, that the God in us can never die. The fact that the world considers a substance harmful or deadly means little to us, since Christ said clearly that one of the signs of His believers is that "if they drink any deadly thing it shall not hurt them" (Mark 16:18). God is stronger than any chemical.

Fear, however, has resulted in laws preventing people from experiencing the effects of certain useful chemicals. Fear has been responsible for depriving mankind of the potential these chemicals have for bringing man into a closer relationship to his brother and to God. . . . Society's laws have made criminals out of people exercising their constitutional right to the pursuit of happiness and peace of mind.

A fundamental principle was discovered in these experiences in breathing: those who breathed from a motivation of giving or helping others were rewarded with a variety of positive experiences. Those who breathed selfishly or greedily, experienced a variety of negative effects. A charitable attitude proved to be essential to a constructive use of these vapors, as did a solid foundation in the Truth of Jesus Christ. The breathing was done only on a voluntary basis, and many of the Church family were discouraged from breathing because of weakness in faith, tendencies toward disobedience, or wrong motivations. Some were asked not to breathe tell-u-all [the Love Family's term for toluene]], because of their immaturity.

The statement also discloses that the church has decided to discontinue the practice of inhaling toluene vapors. Recent reports indicate that the group now engages in another form of breathing exercise — hyperventilating, caused by rapid, deep breathing. Hashish allegedly continues to be used daily.

Karen reported that a hallucinogenic substance was derived from the preparation of a common flower found in their backyard. "They boiled it down to a little paste, and guys had three-day trips on it."

Karen describes another unusual practice of the group: electrical shocks. "They had a cord that you plugged in that had a little metal tube on each end. You would sit around in a circle holding hands, and the person on each end would hold the tube. When the cord was plugged into the wall, the electrical current would pass around the circle. Then one person would drop out, and the circle would get smaller while the current became stronger. The group initially consisted of about twelve people. Eventually the circle would get down to six, five, and even four people. One time it got down to two, and then they got scared because they couldn't get their hands apart, and somebody else had to unplug them."

SHOCKING, IN another sense of that word, was the treatment given some of the children in the Love Family. "Children were not supposed to cry, they were not supposed to be unhappy, they were not supposed to be ungrateful. . . . If they were unhappy they were sent to the closet. Little babies were placed in the closet, and the door closed so we wouldn't have to listen to their screaming. Often, if the child were light enough, he would be picked up by one leg and carried to the closet. That was regular practice involving children from about five months to two years of age. Kids who were used to it and had been at the Family for a long time would just fall asleep in the closet as easily as they would fall asleep anyplace else. But for those who were new, it was a terrifying experience. Generally, when they woke up they would be brought out.

"One little girl who was a year and a half old persisted in being unhappy, which meant she was giving in to Satan. She gave in to Satan instead of accepting Christ, which would have made her happy. One day she was put into a small closet. It was maybe a foot and a half wide and four feet long and dark. She was put in there until she decided to be happy and/or grateful. She stayed in there all day long. She was placed in the closet in the morning right after breakfast and remained there until about seven o'clock at night, when somebody finally decided that she was happy enough. I don't know what she did to make them decide that she was now happy, because she couldn't possibly have been happy in that situation.

"We were taught that Satan works really hard in the children because they are weaker vessels. Therefore the children were to be disciplined severely, because you weren't hurting the children, you were just getting Satan out of their temples. A standard disciplinary measure was to spank the children on their bare bottoms with a stick. They started using a stick, lightly, at the age of five months. Usually the babies would cry, and they would get spanked again. Every house generally had a rod or something they would spank the children with. However, we weren't allowed to spank or punish the children in front of guests. Their reasoning went like this: 'We know it's right, but they don't know that it's right, so we just do it elsewhere.'

"One little guy was really a rebellious kid. He was two and a half years old, and he used to wet his pants. He used to wet the bed all the time, so we made him sleep on the floor, the hard floor, without any blankets. That was really awful."

The rationale for disciplining children originated with Love Israel. "Love told us we had to revise all of our ideas of what love was. He said, 'I am love personified, so whatever I do is loving.'" This meant that former conceptions of loving behavior would take on new meanings. Love's thinking could be summarized as follows: "You might think the best thing to do for a child is to give it tenderness and affection, but in fact that is going to make the child spoiled. It's going to make the child want to control you. You can't give a child what it wants, because then it will learn to want, and you are not supposed to want things. So you just give a child what it needs, and you give it severe discipline, and it will grow up to be strong and grateful."

Another ritual pertained to feeding children not old enough to eat by themselves. "They sat in their chair, and they would have to look at you and not at the food. You would have to hold the food before you gave it to them, and say, 'This is the body of Jesus Christ.' Then you put the food in their mouth. If they reached out for it, you wouldn't give it to them. They weren't allowed to want it, to desire it. Love taught that we really didn't need food. Food was a sacrament and not something that our bodies really need. God will keep our bodies alive. We don't need food."

If a little child acted hungry or made motions toward the food, he was not fed. "One little guy fasted for three days before they finally gave him something to eat.

"When I first came there, the kids didn't have any toys. I used to let them play with spoons. Now they have toys. One of the houses has a playroom, and that's where the children come every day so they can play together."

SEX ROLES were clearly spelled out in the Love Family. There was men's work, and there was women's work. The younger men were expected to help the women with some of their heavy work, like washing clothes. "We washed our clothes by hand or by foot. We would wash them by stomping on them in a tub. Some people scrubbed clothes on a scrub board. There were a couple of washing machines, but there were so many clothes that the washing machines didn't last very long. They just got used and used and used. We hung the clothes out on the line to dry.

"We had nice gardens that were very well kept. There were flowers, fruit trees, and vegetables of all kinds. Most of the heating in the homes came from wood stoves, and the men would go on expeditions to get scrap lumber for the stoves. In the winter the men were expected to shovel paths on the sidewalks between all our houses.

"Generally speaking, the men were not allowed to hold down regular jobs on the outside. I have no idea where the Love Family got its money. We lived by faith, Love said. At one point Love decided that it was all right for us to have a job and earn money if we all did it together. So about three-quarters of the Family went off to eastern Washington to pick cherries."

Love also laid down the rules on marriage and sexual activity within the Family. At one point, celibacy was the norm. "When I first got there, everybody had given up sex until the Marriage Supper of the Lamb. Later Love changed the rules and allowed couples to live as man and wife. A man who wanted to be married would go to Love and would say, 'We would like to get together.' Love made the decision. Sometimes he would notice that two people liked each other, and he would ask, 'Would you two like to live as man and wife?' They would say yes, and they would be 'bonded.' There really wasn't a ceremony — they would just sleep together. Love also had the authority to unbond people. He could say that those two people couldn't sleep together any more. Or, without actually ending the relationship, he could say, 'Well, you are still bonded, but you can't sleep together for now.' And they would obey him.

"One guy got flogged for sleeping with some girl who wasn't in the Family. He wanted to remain in the Family, so he had to submit to a beating as a punishment. He got paddled on his bottom with a stick that was about two feet long — forty swats. Everybody in the Family had to come and watch. One of the elders did the beating, and they hit him pretty hard.

"Very few of the people in the group were bonded. Most people were single. Only those individuals who were very close to Love, who were in top leadership positions, were living together."

Theoretically, Love had sexual access to any woman in the group, according to Karen. "But he didn't take advantage of that privilege. He didn't say, 'You come and stay with me.' That would have freaked me out if he had done that, because I didn't like him very much. I tried to think of him as being a representative of Jesus Christ, but he was kind of a dirty old man."

Karen's life in the Love Family was ordered and regimented. "You never went any place by yourself. You didn't even walk from one house to another by yourself. They told us that when you are by yourself you tend to think; your mind tends to operate, and you don't want to use your mind because 'we are your mind.' Anything your mind tells you is lies. We are your mind and we will tell you truth."

Members of the Love Family are forbidden such worldly luxuries as magazines, newspapers, radios, and television. "We never went to movies. We didn't have television. We didn't need all those worldly things: we had everything we needed right there. We were told that we should be giving things to the world and that we didn't need to take what the world had to offer us."

A TYPICAL day for Karen began at 6:00 A.M. "The women always got up first and fixed the breakfast. While the breakfast was being prepared, we would wake the men up. Every morning we did yoga. Just a few minutes before breakfast we had about a half a dozen exercises that we all did. After breakfast we did the dishes and cleaned up the house. Then we would go out to our various duties. The women would wash clothes and bake bread. After those things were done, you would go and work on some project.

"When I first joined the Family, we had only two meals a day — one at breakfast and one about 4:30 in the afternoon. Just before I left, they started having three meals a day: a light breakfast, a dinner at lunch, and a snack in the evening. After the main meal in mid-afternoon, you had free time. I would sometimes sew or draw. I got so that I just thought about food all the time. I would just hang around hoping that I wouldn't miss a snack in the evening.

"On the Sabbath everybody always got dressed up in their best dresses. Usually we went over to Love's house. We usually spent the whole day over there and had a big dinner all together, the whole Family. We would just lie around and talk. That was always very pleasant. There were several musical groups in the Family, and on the Sabbath they would play music. And they were good, too. They wrote most of their own music. It was all about the Family; it was all religious music. We sang a few songs from the outside, but they were censored to make sure they didn't go against any of the teachings of the Family.

"Every day we had something like devotions around the meal table. They considered that everything we ate and drank was communion. The household elders would lead the conversation, and occasionally Love would read from Scripture. Mostly he just talked. He would speak about the virtue of being in the Family and how we all were such creeps before we joined the Family and how now we are such godly people.

"For a while during my stay, we would meet every morning at Love's house. We would all crowd in, and he would talk and talk. I thought it was real boring. He wasn't a charismatic speaker. But he did have rather clever methods for making people believe. He had a way of asking questions and selecting certain people to give testimonies so that the positive aspects of the Family would be highlighted."

A neophyte member was encouraged to "give everything up to God," which really meant giving everything over to Love

Israel. He was viewed as the administrator of the body of Christ. The church charter reads, "Members of the Church of Armageddon will give all they possess to the Church upon joining." This was based on the biblical injunction found in Acts 2: "And all that believed were together, and they had all things common; they sold their possession and goods, and parted them to all men, as every man had need."

Karen signed a statement assigning everything to the church and giving the church the right to sign her old name on checks. "I don't know if it was a binding document or not, but I signed it anyway. You were supposed to give what was yours, and if people wanted to give you things, then you gave them to the Love Family. A lot of things people gave ended up being ornaments in Love's house. I had a real good harmonica that I really liked, and it got sold. Love also had a big harmonica, and his didn't get sold, and that made me mad."

WHY WAS Love Israel permitted to exercise such power over the lives of people? What kind of people needed or wanted that kind of authoritarian direction?

Karen feels that many of the men, especially, were indebted to Love because of very real changes he was able to effect in their lives. "Some of the men who were there had been real losers in their life earlier, and he had brought them in, he had opened his doors to them. These people were really outcasts, entirely insecure, and he had really built them into men. They were honestly grateful. They were just filled with gratitude to him. He represented something of a model to them. Many of the individuals at the Love Family came there from a problem situation. They were looking for some kind of structure. I think my generation is looking for structure. He was a man with all the answers. You knew that you didn't know the truth. He said, 'I do.' He was in control.

"The first year I was there, we had a big Christmas party at Love's house, and everybody had to take off their clothes before they went in. He said, 'Take off your clothes,' and everybody did. But Love wore a towel the whole time.

"We considered ourselves a nation, a kingdom. Love was the king. He was in fact anointed King, a few years earlier."

"There was one boy named Happiness who always talked about the king. Happiness was definitely a loyal subject in everything he did. He once said, 'I would jump off a cliff if Love asked me to.'

"We were to serve Love and make him the center of our attention. The idea was that if you gave all of your love to Love, some of it would spill over to everybody else. Most of the people considered themselves to be his servants, his guardians. There were a lot of people there who would do anything for Love."

THE MAIN office of the Love Family is located in an old storefront on West McGraw Street in Seattle. The office is kept open twenty-four hours a day. During the night, three or four people are "on watch" in case of visitors. Twice each night, Karen says, two of these nocturnal watchmen would "do the circuit" — make the rounds of all the Love Family houses in the immediate area. A bizarre aspect of this was that the watchmen would awaken each member. Karen explains why: "They would ask you if God was giving you any dreams or visions. If someone was having a bad dream, they would try to counsel the person and be of assistance if they were frightened. Also, it provided an opportunity to tell each member in the middle of the night that they were loved and appreciated. Love encouraged people to write down their visions."

Members were not, however, encouraged to use physicians or hospitals. "We didn't believe in disease. If you got sick, it was a sign of your lack of faith. At one particular time, most members of the Family came down with some kind of illness, and we did as little as possible to indicate that we had it. At most, occasionally we took more naps."

Karen also reports that people threw away their glasses, because eyeglasses were another sign that you lacked faith. One young woman had difficulty seeing someone across the table when she removed her glasses. Within a few days of her arrival, the elders had her believing that as her faith grew, she would be able to see.

Occasionally the entire Family would go down to a local

playing field and march in formation. In Karen's opinion, this was done to keep members physically fit and to reinforce the practice of obeying orders. "Sometimes we would have to march double time. I was pregnant at the time and had to keep up with the group."

KAREN'S PARENTS made the decision to have her abducted from the cult. Interestingly, she did not resist. "It just seemed like a scene out of a movie. I concluded that whatever would happen, it would be God's will."

Karen feels that the abduction and deprograming were fully justified and necessary. "I would never have left on my own. You couldn't have talked me out. No way!"

◆ FIVE ◆

The Unification Church

SHELLEY LIEBERT is a bright, articulate, sophisticated young woman who, like many of her peers, sampled a number of the options available to young people in today's society — including travel. "I traveled abroad, and when I returned home, I decided that I wanted to lead the life of a normal, average girl. I didn't want to be a gypsy any more. So I got a job as a secretary, and I lived at home, and I was making an effort to be as normal as I could.

"For a few years prior to this time, I'd been struggling with my feelings about Christianity — I come from a Jewish family. When I had visited Greece, which is a very religious nation, I felt it was okay to be a Christian. Then, when I was back home, I discovered it wasn't okay, and there was a big struggle going on. So under cover I joined a Christian church. I locked myself in the bathroom, and I took the Yellow Pages, and I looked up a church, went there, and said, 'I want to be baptized.' It was a Greek Orthodox church, because I was really turned off by anything that was the slightest bit fanatical. I didn't want to 'praise the Lord,' I just wanted to be a good person. And I was attracted to the tradition of the Greek Orthodox Church.

"All this time I was lying to my mother, telling her I was going out with my boyfriend when I was really going to church. The tension just built up, and I thought, 'How can I lie? How can I lie before God? I can't live a double life any more.' The struggle was becoming more intense, and I was thinking — always in absolutes — 'Either I tell my mother, or I'm going to have to run away and become a nun.' That's the way I looked at life. There was no in-between.

"I tried to make an appointment with a priest, but he was always out to lunch with the bishop. I wanted to talk to him about entering a convent. Just at this time, when the struggle was the greatest, I met the Moonies. In the section of Los Angeles where I worked, when you walk down the street you are assaulted by the Children of God, Scientology, or some other religious group. At that particular time, Rev. Moon was going to give a speech at the Schubert Theater, and many of his people were walking around with big placards. I didn't particularly want to talk to them. But one day I was approached by someone who wasn't wearing a placard.

"It was the last day of the year, and on the last day of each year, all the secretaries take those little flip calendars out of their holders and let them drop from the office buildings. All over the city these 'days' were falling down on the streets. I was feeling very melancholy, just watching the whole year at my feet. I thought to myself, 'This is my life every year. This is the last day of the year. I have to do one thing or another.' And that's when I met them.

"I'd never heard anything about the Unification Church before. I thought they were just an international Christian youth group. They invited me to a weekend retreat. During that weekend — it seemed like a hundred years rather than two days — the transition was made. In that one weekend I made up my mind to join. This seemed to be the perfect solution to a life of devotion which wouldn't cut me off from the rest of the world. It seemed to me that this is what God wanted me to do.

"The people from the Unification Church struck me as being devoted and very civilized. Very clean-cut, very purposeful, and very kind. I was impressed. This particular group of Moonies was largely European, and I have always been impressed by European people. Because they were religious and European, it somehow all fit together.

"During the weekend workshop we heard a lot of lectures. I can remember thinking, 'This is really crazy.' But I was very impressed with the lecturer. He was German, and I really liked the way he presented his points. I was impressed with the hierarchy and the kind of people who were leading the workshop. We were at a YMCA camp and were all grubby, yet they were always clean. They somehow never seemed to get tired. They were always very civilized. They identified themselves as the One World Crusade, and they had me convinced that this thing was sweeping the world and that I had just found out about it. They gave the impression that the rest of the world was also finding out about it at the very same moment.

"At the conclusion of the weekend, I went home and quit my job. Several days of personal struggle followed, and at one point I didn't really want to go back to their organization. I remember sitting with my mom, my suitcases packed, and saying, 'I don't want to go.' But I had left a sleeping bag at the camp and I knew that I had to at least go get that sleeping bag. Anyway, I was just going to go for a seven-day program, and at the end of that time I would re-evaluate it and see if this is what I wanted to do. So I made up my mind to go through with it. As soon as my parents dropped me off at the camp, that was it. From that point on, I was embraced by a new life, a new situation."

THE NEW life upon which Shelley was about to embark would be molded by a church founded in Seoul, Korea, in 1954 and known as "The Holy Spirit Association for the Unification of World Christianity." More commonly known as simply the Unification Church, this religious cult is also identified by many other names, or "fronts," including One World Crusade, which Shelley joined. Other organizations under the Unification umbrella include the International Cultural Foundation, Creative Community Project, D. C. Striders Track Club, Collegiate Association for the Research of Principles (CARP), Korean Folk Ballet, Unification Thought Institute, Council for Unified Research and Education, and New Hope Singers International. The basic stated objective of the Moon Church is to bring happiness, new hope, and unification to a world in despair and change. A brochure prepared by the organization states, "More than ever, we can see that the ultimate solution to the human crisis and conflict cannot come from man's created institutions or from man alone. Many expect that this is the time when God will reveal new truth (John 16:25) — truth higher than existing religions or ideologies — to solve the fundamental questions of human life and to lead man to a new world of harmony and peace."

The one man who is said to be able to bring "new hope" to this "new age" is Sun Myung Moon, Korean-born evangelist, millionaire, industrialist, and founder of the Unification Church. Born in North Korea to Presbyterian parents in 1920, Moon started praying for "extraordinary things" when he was just twelve years old. On Easter morning in 1936, Moon was praying on a Korean mountainside when Jesus Christ is said to have appeared to him and told him that he had been selected to carry out an important mission. Moon relates that he was asked to assume the responsibility of completing Christ's "unfinished" task. He was sixteen years old then and spent the next nine years in prayer and deep study. During this time, a series of principles was revealed to Moon that resulted in his being able to understand clearly the nature of the universe, the meaning of history, and the "inner meanings" of the biblical parables and symbols. A pamphlet published by the Unification Church describes it this way: "The revelation was received progressively through prayer, study of all religious scriptures, meditation, spiritual communication with such persons as Jesus, Moses and Buddha, and direct communication with God. At the end of this time, Reverend Moon had been led by God to solve the vast spiritual puzzle, and was now ready to bring this revelation to the world."

In 1965 Moon embarked on his first world tour, traveling to forty countries, including the United States. Four years later he again visited the United States, speaking to audiences in seven major cities. This public speaking tour is considered the formal beginning of his ministry in America. In 1973 the controversial cult leader moved his headquarters to the United States, where he now has over thirty thousand followers and over five thousand core members who live in over 120 communal centers and training camps.

Moon is hailed as a modern-day prophet and spiritual leader "with a truly international vision." Publicly his followers are reluctant to identify him as the messiah. Once a person joins the Unification Church, however, it becomes clear that Moon is, in fact, regarded as "the Messiah, the Lord of the Second Advent."

Shelley recalls that she didn't hear about the messiah for the first two or three weeks. "I saw his picture. I didn't make any association, and then one night they were showing slides and everything seemed to fit together. About three weeks after I joined, I came to the conclusion, 'He must be the messiah. . . .'

"All the leaders in my camp were German. My mother was German, so that was a link for me. She had brought us up to feel that we were better than Americans: we were cultured. We were raised on Mozart. And so I resonated with these leaders. I could speak German with them and no one else would understand. I could be elite.

"They were very regimented in schedule and in dress. They were completely formal at all times. I became so conditioned that if I saw a man without a tie on, it was like seeing him naked. If something started at six o'clock, you had better be there at exactly six, when the doors were closed and locked. Everything was exactly on time, very German."

SHELLEY COMPLETED the seven-day seminar and went on to the twenty-one-day training program. She never quite completed the latter, however, because of a pressing need for new workers in the field. "We were sent out to work right away. I tried several different things. I was witnessing for a while and fund-raising for a while; then they sent me up to the camp to be an assistant to the instructor."

Shelley's intelligence and leadership qualities were soon recognized by the leaders, and she was asked to assume the role of an instructor on short notice. She was given only three days to study the *Divine Principle*, the book (first published in 1957) containing Moon's revelations and the basic doctrines of the Unification Church. "I was really nervous because I had to lecture right from the book. Whatever I felt was true, I just threw in. Eventually, through discussion with other teachers, I got to learn the *Divine Principle* more and more."

The leadership at the camp consisted of between ten and twenty persons, depending on the number of "trainees" in residence at the workshop at any given time. The camp population would vary from a low of twenty to as many as one hundred. The new recruits were there for various seminars lasting three days, seven days, or twenty-one days. The longer seminars represent something of a progression in the dispensing of knowledge and doctrine, an unfolding of information. Shelley pointed out, however, that at times the twenty-one-day session would be curtailed because of the need to raise funds. In that case, lectures were given in the van while on the move or after returning to the camp at night.

According to Shelley, new trainees always arrived at the camp in the middle of the night — by design. "It's a winding, dark road, and they usually fell asleep in the van. By the time they got there, they were completely disoriented. Most of them are not prepared for what is going to happen. They don't know where they're going to sleep, what the arrangement is going to be like. Then they are placed in a dorm, the men's dorm or the women's dorm.

"New trainees are up by 7:00 A.M. There's a time of prayer at 7:30, and by eight o'clock sharp they have to be on the volleyball courts for exercises. These are optional activities, but the peer pressure is strong and everyone participates. For us, the exercise period included singing and joking, all with a religious undertone, in order to release any feelings of tension that we were narrow-minded about religion. We developed our own routines and cheers. Whatever worked the first time, we used the second time and then over and over again. After a year of doing it, I became so sick of those routines: I knew exactly what costume to come on in and when it was going to happen. We had the whole thing choreographed. Whatever did the trick, we used, and whatever didn't do the trick, we threw out. The whole purpose was to put the hook in, to discover what would grab them emotionally, to find ways to make them feel that at last they were home. We wanted to communicate that they had nothing more to fear, that they were among friends. We understood them completely. All the love that they had ever wanted was now theirs.

"Exercise was followed by breakfast, and then immediately classes began. There were lectures (with a mid-morning break) until lunch time, at 12:30 or 1:00 P.M. After lunch we had sports, volleyball, and hikes. I usually loved hiking, because we would walk down the mountain to the lake and then back again. Sometimes, when it was very hot and I was exhausted, I nevertheless had to act like I was enjoying it. We had to always set an example, so the leaders have to be more enthusiastic than anyone else. Sometimes I really felt like an army matron.

"After sports we would resume lectures until dinner time. After dinner, lectures again until 11:00 P.M., or group discussion, or once in a great while we had an evening activity — like a variety show during which everyone would get up and sing and give testimonies. At the end of the day the trainees would go back to their dorms and talk among themselves.

"Every day was a very full day. You are always given more to do than you can possibly accomplish. There is always studying to do. If trainees wanted to keep up with what the lectures were about, they had to stay up later and study. I think in that kind of a situation, there is enough of an emotional and physical strain so that even six hours of sleep is short.

"All the physical activity helped to build a sense of the group, a 'we' feeling. We also had a lot of informal talks on the porch. We shared the feeling that we had been misunderstood by society and now we were among friends. We felt that God understood us and that He had actually prepared us throughout the course of human history — prepared our ancestors — that we might come to this point in history. Every failure that we might have had in our lives was a reinforcement of the idea of God's divine leading, because now we could view it all as a victory in preparation for enduring persecution or suffering."

SHELLEY POINTS out that the group capitalizes on the search for love that many new recruits experience. She describes the instructor-trainee role as a form of parent-child relationship. "That was my role, to be very motherly or very wifely or sisterly. The teacher was the parent who would substitute for Moon, who was the True Parent. It was always a parent-child relationship. The people I brought into the group even called me 'mom.' And they were my 'sons' and 'daughters' whom I provided for physically and emotionally. I represented a

shoulder to cry on. For the instructor, that filled a tremendous
need to be a parent, to have that kind of control; to be a trainee
filled a need to be a child, to be supported and encouraged and
comforted.

"There was always stress on what they called vertical
relationships and horizontal relationships. The vertical relationship would be with God or someone in God's position —
your superior or those people below you. Horizontal relationships were taboo: they were considered worldly. The only time
you were allowed to develop horizontal relationships was
when you were qualified. The scriptural support for this idea
was Jesus' command that we love God (the First Commandment) — the vertical relationship. You could only love your
brother after having achieved the first relationship. Then you
were qualified.

"We were taught that the Fallen Nature of Man has four
aspects. The first is the failure to see things from God's point of
view: you always had to see things from God's standpoint, and
the only representative of God you had was your superior.
Whether he's right or wrong, you follow his orders. If he's made
mistakes in his command, then he's the one that has to pay for it
and not you. So you follow without question, you follow God's
representative.

"The second aspect of the Fallen Nature involves leaving
one's proper position. Lucifer left his original position in order
to fulfill his selfish desires. You were told that you had to
remain in your position. There is always a subject-object relationship, a superior-inferior relationship.

"Thirdly, the Fallen Nature involves a reversal of dominion. The implication is that if you questioned a superior, you
had to fast or pray before you even opened your mouth. One
of the worst things you could do was to go over someone's
head.

"The fourth characteristic of the Fallen Nature has to do
with the multiplication of sin. Supposedly, Lucifer seduced
Eve, and Eve seduced Adam. That was a transfer of sin. In the
Moonies, the worst thing you can do is to get two people
together so that they can multiply sin. All horizontal relationships were supposed to be severed. If an instructor ever saw two

people talking together, that was their opportunity to multiply sin. So you had to be sure to separate them. This even applied to close relationships between members of the same sex. If you saw two girls together, you had to separate them.

"I was always being reprimanded because I was being too 'horizontal.' We were supposed to love people, so I cared about whatever it was they were needing. If they wanted to talk about their problems with their girl friend, I didn't care. So I was getting into trouble because I became too involved in their lives."

DURING PART of her sojourn in the Unification Church, Shelley worked in Mr. Moon's personal mansion in Pasadena. This luxurious estate constitutes his private headquarters on the West Coast. "We were taught that the planet Earth was at the center of the cosmos and that God had struggled all this time to create America. Within America there were two special locations — Los Angeles and New York. They were considered to be equally important. Within Los Angeles there was a spiritual center — the house in which I worked. And I was the housekeeper; I filled a kind of mother role. My job was considered extremely important. The mansion was also the place where the Moon public relations people stayed. My job was to cook and clean for the public relations girls. It was sort of like being Cinderella. I didn't get to be one because I guess I didn't fit the image. You have to be able to go out and mingle with the mayor and have a certain kind of personality. I just didn't have the glow of health that was required.

"These girls had quite an expense account, and they would only work for a few hours each day. They would get up late and go out for a few hours and tell me how exhausted they were. And I was up till 3:30 every morning ironing their clothes and scrubbing the floors and cooking their meals. I didn't have any help. Anytime some of the officials, like Colonel Pak or Mrs. Choi, would fly in from Korea, I'd have to have their rooms prepared. Everything had to be done with the correct spiritual attitude: if it wasn't prepared that way, it wasn't acceptable. It wasn't enough to just iron their clothes; it had to be done with a prayerful heart. I really hated them. When anything went wrong in the community, it reflected my attitude.

"They would lord it over me, and they knew just how to get me. I couldn't say anything. They would always bring up the example of Mrs. Kang, a Korean woman who was associated with the Moonies for about twenty-five years — and she was still peeling potatoes and scrubbing floors after twenty-five years. . . . She trained me for this job. She never complained, never said a word.

"When things started to go bad, it was my fault. One day our Regional Director took me into a room and sat me down. He said, 'Shelley, do you realize you should be very glad that God doesn't come and judge you right now. If he did, you'd really be in sorry shape.' I said, 'Okay.' Mind you, I'm holding up half of America. I'm the female Atlas. He said, 'Do you realize that you're responsible for bringing Satan into this house?' I felt like Judas; I was going to go hang myself. But I knew it wouldn't do any good, because then I would just go into the spiritual world, and you'd have to pay all that indemnity in the spirit world. Sometimes I was just crying from sheer exhaustion and hatred and confusion. I knew that the more I did that, the more I was responsible for the downfall of America. We were really convinced that everything we did had direct effect on the world. Like when Mao Tse-tung died, I'm sure everyone felt it had something to do with them.

"If anything went wrong, I always felt that I was personally responsible. Because I was the housekeeper, I was responsible for the atmosphere in the home: I set the tone, like a wife."

ONE DAY Shelley met the Korean messiah in person. "I was trained for three months to know how to serve him. We spent many hours a day praying in preparation for his visit. It's impossible to pray that long: you have to go into sort of a trance. We would conjure up his image in our minds. I knew his face better than I knew my own. By the way, I never looked in a mirror: I never had an opportunity to. I knew his face so well, and I loved him so much! I thought about him all the time! I was thrilled for the opportunity to be the housekeeper, because that meant I would get to personally care for him.

"Preparations for his coming were elaborate. The entire

kitchen had to be cleaned out — everything had to be taken out. Everything had to be replaced. If you wanted to use a particular canned good, you had to buy the biggest and most expensive. Even if you had a can which was not opened, you still had to buy a new one. Everything had to be completely new. After all, you were preparing it for 'God.'

"If you wanted to use an onion, you would buy a crate of onions and pick out the best one. When he and his entourage arrived, we had to place fruit in each room. One of the guests arrived early and there wasn't fruit in his room, so I quickly picked out some fruit and put it in his room — I was scolded and told to put it back. The first fruit that was taken out had to be for Mr. Moon. After that, other fruit could be taken out. He always got the best portion.

"Everything was washed. If you washed a banana, you had to use Q-Tips. It had to be washed not only physically, but also spiritually. The resulting bowl of fruit is very beautiful: it really shines, and it has to be arranged just perfectly. Everything was prepared and stacked in a certain way.

"I had to go to all the Korean markets and learn the names of strange dishes and how to prepare them. . . . We bought everything that he could possibly think of needing. I had to call long-distance to New York to find out what kind of underwear he used. I would even have dreams about the doormat not being new. I felt guilty about spending money, because I knew how hard the kids worked to raise it. Yet we were told that it was okay to buy anything. You had to buy things even though you knew he wouldn't need them. Like he doesn't drink coffee, but you had to buy a coffee pot anyway. It was very much like a Passover, when you buy everything new.

"Finally the big day arrived. I had everything down pat. I knew where to put his slippers — on the right side or the left side. I knew that when you offered something to him, you had to use both hands — it was considered impolite to use one hand. Then you would bow and step back three steps before turning to walk away.

"There's so much preparation involved with oriental food, because it has so many ingredients. Every single thing you did had to be done with the correct attitude. While chopping the garlic, if you weren't praying, he[Moon] would know. We were always told that if you weren't prayerful enough, he wouldn't eat the food.

"While praying, you had to encompass all of human history, all of human thought and feeling. You had to think of everything, you were supposed to pray for everyone all the time. But you couldn't pray for Moon, just like you wouldn't pray for Jesus: it was inappropriate. We would pray for the people around him that they might serve him well.

"WHEN MR. MOON arrived, he didn't acknowledge me at all. When I served his dinner, nothing! We were all running around like crazy. I had been up for three days, with less than an hour's sleep each day. We had to keep the kitchen spotless. But because of the way Orientals cook, it was impossible: they bring in a big bin of vegetables, and they chop it up, and the parts they don't want they just throw on the floor. It was a mess — a lot of oil, ox tails, deep fat frying, everything was splattering.

"My mother lived about three miles down the road from the mansion. She had come one time before to the house, and I was deathly afraid that she might come during Moon's visit. But I felt this spiritual force surrounding the place so that no evil would be able to penetrate. God and all the angels would be there. There would be no danger of anyone coming near the spiritual barrier.

"Moon had a certain magnificence about him. When he walked into the room, you felt blown against the wall. He had an invisible force around him. You felt that if someone were to shoot him, the bullet would swerve. You couldn't approach him or touch anything that he had touched without the right attitude. There was a mystique, almost mythology, about him. We were told that whenever he went to the zoo, all the animals would run over to that part of the zoo. When he visited a fish pond, all the fish would swim over to him. He had dominion over creation, and I felt that every leaf, every grain of sand, was truly waiting for his presence.

"Mr. Moon's wife looked at me like I was the stable boy. She felt so sorry for me. She looked at me as if to say, 'Oh God, you poor kid.' She gave me a necklace, and everyone thought,

'Wow! The Mother gave you a necklace.' I gave it to somebody else because I didn't think it was that precious.

"One day Moon became very upset because I was wearing an orange apron. Apparently he only liked white and gold. For some reason, orange is just really not acceptable. I was splattered with grease, and I had to put on something — I put the orange apron on, and he was furious.

"The night of his arrival, everyone was exhausted and all the members went to bed. I thought, *How can they sleep when Father is in the house?* I was the only one to stay up all night. I spent all night praying and making breakfast. When he didn't eat my breakfast, I was crushed. He wouldn't touch it, I reasoned, because my thought wasn't pure. I think he just wanted a cup of tea, and that was it.

"Moon's stay in Pasadena was very brief. After he had left, all of the things he had used and touched were divided up among the members. They were considered to be sacred artifacts to be preserved for posterity, like splinters from the cross.

"After he left, I just collapsed from exhaustion. I locked myself in the library of the mansion and cried and cried for hours. I cried because I felt that he was the embodiment of all the love that could possibly be. I was crying tears of joy: everything in history had been funneled down to this one man, and I was connected to him. I thought about him constantly; I pictured him always; everything I thought about was somehow connected to him."

SUCH STATEMENTS of adoration and devotion are clear evidence that Shelley and thousands of true believers like her saw in Moon the markings of a messiah. How does this missionary from Korea view himself? What lies behind the strange pull of Mr. Moon? His own words, spoken in 1965 to a group of followers, give a clue:

> I have certain things you can find nowhere else. This is what has drawn you to me. What might seem presumptuous does not trouble me. My conscience is all clear and happy. You *owe* me. Without me there is a certain distance you cannot go in your search for God. You *must* come to

Him through me. You are following the universal path to
heaven which has been sent by me.

Members of the Unification Church refer to Reverend Moon as
"Father" or "Master." In a talk to his leaders in January 1973, he
referred to himself as "the prophet of prophets." In the same
speech he referred to the inadequacies of past saints, prophets,
religious leaders, and theologians, and concluded, "Master is
more than any of those people and greater than Jesus himself."
Later in the same talk, he suggested that he is a kind of spiritual
physician: "You are in the position of the diseased, and you
need a physician, and Master is in that position. If you are a
patient with an incurable disease — almost hopeless — would
you not obey your physician in order to be cured?"

On still another occasion, Moon, filled with delusions of
messianic grandeur, observed, "The time will come, without
my seeking it, that my words will almost serve as law. If I ask a
certain thing, it will be done. If I don't want something, it will
not be done."

When he made his first trip to the United States, Sun
Myung Moon was virtually unknown. "I came to America
bare-handed. However, when I moved in, things started happening, not only here in America, but all over the world." One
of the places where things first started happening was in the
real estate market. Moon, his wife, and eight children live in a
twenty-five-room mansion on an estate purchased for $620,000
in suburban Westchester County, New York. The church also
owns the twenty-two-acre Belvedere estate in Tarrytown, New
York, valued at $850,000. The movement's training center is
located in a former Christian Brothers Seminary in Barrytown
purchased for $1,500,000. The cult also bought the former
Columbia University Club for $1.2 million, and more recently
acquired the forty-two-story former New Yorker Hotel for $5
million. The latter has been transformed into the world headquarters of the Unification Church.

Mr. Moon's financial empire, including extensive industrial holdings in Korea, is said to be worth at least $15 million.
His organization has been criticized for the fund-raising
methods employed by his thousands of youthful followers in
the United States. That he is using the enthusiasm and energy

of his followers to enrich the coffers of his church is obvious from the following candid comments made to a group of his core leaders in 1973:

> Even in the Communistic army they are financially sup-ported. They are given food, clothing, arms — but I am going to use you, trying to get money out of you. Are you ready to follow that kind of a leader? You must be crazy people. I am sure you know that, if I am going to do that at all, I am not going to do that for my own sake. I have everything with me to support myself. I have earned quite a sum of money on which I can live all through my life. Some 13 million dollars I have earned. With that, I can lead a well-to-do life. That money I have deposited in the bank, but I have bought land for you to use in the future for international training centers to build and I have estab-lished factories to make more money for the movement. When I am telling you to make your own livelihood and even send back some of the money to the Headquarters, I am not doing that for my sake, you well know that I am going to do that for the sake of saving the world. Even dictators like Hitler, when he utilized the people, he had to financially support them. Even Stalin had to financially support the people when he used them. But here I am, as the leader of this group, and I am going to use you by being paid! In that case I am the only example of that in the whole world in all human history. Am I not? Still, do you want to follow me?

SHELLEY WAS willingly "used" by the Unification Church in its efforts to obtain financial support. "I went on a fund-raising team into New Mexico and Arizona with new trainees. The first time I was put on a fund-raising team, I didn't make it. I quit. It was the only time I didn't do what I was told. One morning I just refused to go, because it was so traumatic. But this time, be-cause I was an instructor, I had to set an example for the new trainees. I had to make the most money.

"We were in New Mexico, and it was very cold, freezing cold. We had to be in the van by 6:00 P.M., and we didn't get back until 3:00 or 3:30 in the morning. Sometimes we stayed out all night. Our team leader was an ex-marine: he really drove us and pushed us. We were literally instructed to run. If you ever got tired, you had to outrun Satan. While riding in the van, we would have what was called a 'shout-out': we'd roll down all the windows while driving along the highway and scream as loud as we could. This was part of building a team spirit. And you always wanted to be the first one out of the van. So when the team leader would pull into a lot and ask, 'Who wants out?' everyone's hand would hit the ceiling.

"I developed a problem with one of my legs. A black line appeared on the leg, and it increased to the point where I couldn't move my leg any more. The driver pulled the van over to the side of the road and got into the back. I was lying on the bench, the first seat. He started pounding on my leg to get the spirits out of my leg — it didn't improve. Eventually it got so bad that I was crossing the street and my leg just stopped. There was a fire station across the street, and one of the firemen came out, and I asked, 'Would you be so kind as to lean me up against this wall across the street?' I was leaning up against the wall, and I was determined to give it a real spartan chance. I started hallucinating and was pretty frightened. When people would appear, I wouldn't see a person, I'd see an image — like a Dr. Seuss character. I'd see elephants and rhinoceroses. I hallucinated like that for a few hours and then I blacked out. That was the very last experience that I had fund-raising."

Shelley's experience is reminiscent of a statement that Moon made to a group of leaders in which he stressed the rewards that come even with adversity. After a hard day's work, he pointed out, their legs might indeed become painful: "Even though you have sore legs, you will be happy and satisfied for what you have done. You may have to groan in bed for the pain you feel in your legs, but you are grateful for what you have done and God will love you."

Shelley recalls one evening when two new trainees had a very traumatic experience. The mobile unit had been selling candy, and at the end of the evening when the van picked up the fund-raisers, two of the young men had not sold the desired quota. "They just couldn't sell any more. And to come back with your box of candy still full was very humiliating. We were all singing a song, and one boy — Tim — and the other boy — Tony — weren't singing. Our team leader, or captain — you never call them by their first name — asked them to sing. They wouldn't sing. There's a Korean cheer that we used which, translated, means 'Victory to Father.' He asked them to shout that cheer, and they wouldn't do it. Tim had these big tears rolling down his cheek, his head was down, and he just wouldn't budge. So the captain pulled the van over to the side of the road onto a big vacant field. He ordered everyone out of the van — something he would often do just to keep us on our toes. He ordered everyone out, and we had to run. It was in the middle of the night and freezing cold, and we were all exhausted. We ran and ran, and then he stopped us and put us in a circle and demanded that Tim shout the cheer. But Tim couldn't do it. Then he made us run again. We did this over and over until Tim finally said the cheer in a whisper. But that wasn't good enough. We were all tired, and Tim knew that we were suffering for his sake. So finally he just screamed — it chills my blood to think of it! It was like all hell broke loose. He just screamed at the top of his lungs. He was broken. We got back into the van and drove off.

"We were told that the best Moonie fund-raiser was a girl whose knees both went out and who lost her voice. The message was clearly that it didn't matter what your physical condition was: if you had the correct, prayerful attitude, people would appear out of nowhere. The legendary fund-raiser reported that if she was dropped off in a vacant field, she would simply pray and run in circles and cars would appear out of nowhere. She would completely sell out."

SOUTHERN CALIFORNIA Moonies are given a mimeographed, three-page list of fund-raising suggestions. Several model sales pitches are presented, including one in Spanish. Recruits are instructed to "memorize them or develop your own, depending upon which feels the most comfortable to use and brings the best results." One sample sales pitch goes this way:

> Good morning! I'm fundraising for our camp in the San Bernadino mountains for rehabilitating young people. We have about 70 people up there at times and it costs a lot of money to maintain it. Could you help us out and buy a box of candy?
>> note: a) they should ask the cost of the candy at this point; respond, "$2.00."

b) if they are extremely negative or give you a firm "no," just ask for a donation.
c) if they seem uncertain about buying or are reluctant to pay $2/box continue. . . .

We just purchased our camp from the YMCA about one year ago and we're trying to meet our expenses. Most of the people who come to our camp don't have a lot of money so our fundraising efforts cover most of the costs. Couldn't you help us out and buy just one box of candy?

> note: continue talking until the person indicates he is interested in buying a box of candy; or if he is not interested just ask for a donation.

If the contact turns out to be a diabetic or indicates that two dollars a box is too expensive, the fund-raiser is told to explain, "The money is a donation to help people; the candy is just a gift to show our appreciation." Additional hints on how to raise money include —

Stay centered on God and your mission and pray frequently in True Parents' [Moon and his wife] name. Before counting your money in evening offer your sacrifice for the day to God in the name of True Parents.

Always try to sell your candy "3 for $5"; this is a golden line. It works especially well going shop to shop as you lay 3 boxes in front of the customer.

Always always ask for a donation if the person is not interested in buying candy. You can increase your results by 10% to 15% during the day if you are consistent about this.

Do not witness to the people while you are fundraising. If someone looks very substantial try to get their phone # or address and call them your first opportunity.

Do not allow yourself to get spiritually low. Avoid lengthy conversations with people who are very negative. Cut off the conversation as quickly as possible or they will drain your spirit for the day and you will have to pay much indemnity to restore your spirit.

Avoid upsetting the customer; if the person does not buy candy from you be polite and cheerful and this will lay a foundation for the next person to make a sale.

Dress neatly and have your hair well groomed; people will often judge you by your external appearance. When dealing with the public it is very important to establish a high standard in this area.

If you run out of candy buy "Kraker Jack" [sic] and sell it for $1/box.

Always address a person as "Sir" or "Miss" — this is a very subtle form of flattery.

If possible try to get the perspective [sic] customer to hold a box of candy; many people find it difficult to return the candy once they've had an opportunity to hold it.

Love the candy you are trying to sell, unite with it and try to convey this feeling to the customer.

Unity with your team and team captain is of utmost importance. Pray for one another frequently during the day.

We accept food stamps as payment for our candy. Also, if a person tells you he has no money chances are he has his check book with him. Tell him "We accept personal checks" and they may feel compelled to buy a box.

A typical Moonie fund-raiser brings in between one and five hundred dollars a day. Two hundred dollars a day is probably about average. A team will sometimes begin as early as nine in the morning and work until past midnight. Many different items are sold to raise money, including carnations, peanuts, and candy. Shelley reports, "One of the fund-raising teams I managed ran out of products, so they went to Avis Rent-a-Car and got those little buttons that say 'We try harder,' and sold those. It didn't matter what you sold. Sometimes we didn't even take the price tag off. It was marked thirty-nine cents, and we would sell it for two dollars. We would buy products in a grocery store and resell them in their own parking lot. Many times people would say, 'You're not working for Moon, are you?' I'd say, 'Oh, no.' They'd give me two dollars. That's an example of 'heavenly deception.'"

REVEREND MOON has been strongly criticized because of his own affluent life style. He justifies the expenditure of large sums of money on the grounds that it's all for the good of the Unification Church. Speaking to a group of followers at Tarrytown, he once said:

In this rather materialistic country, I thought that we must have something to show. That is why I bought the estate. And in the future, when I invite to my home Senators and Congressmen and many V.I.P.'s from many nations, I feel I must show them other than the miserable side of life. That is also why I bought a luxurious car. Not for myself. In my everyday life, if possible, I choose not to ride in that luxurious car. When I do, I do it for the dignity of the Unification Church, and usually when I take my people with me.

Every Sunday morning at exactly five o'clock, members of the Unification Church assemble for what is called a "pledge" service. "You can't be a moment late," Shelley notes. "Men have to wear suits, women wear dresses — their Sunday best. The men are seated on the left side of the room, the women on the right side. In the front of the room is a small table on which fresh flowers have been placed. Also, on a doily there is a picture of Moon. The service begins with the leader, always a man, directing the group to bow down three times to the heavenly Father and the True Parents. You place your right hand over your left hand, and you put your hands on your forehead and bow down to the floor. You put your forehead on the floor. This is repeated three times. Then everyone recites the following pledge in unison:

> As the center of the cosmos, I will fulfill our Father's Will [purpose of creation], and the responsibility given me [for self-perfection]. I will become a dutiful son [or daughter] and a child of goodness to attend our Father forever in the ideal world of creation [by] returning joy and glory to Him. This I pledge.
>
> I will take upon myself completely the Will of God to give me the whole creation as my inheritance. He has given me His Word, His personality, and His heart, and is reviving me who had died, making me one with Him and His true child. To do this, our Father has persevered for 6,000 years the sacrificial way of the cross. This I pledge.
>
> As a true son [or daughter], I will follow our Father's pattern and charge bravely forward into the enemy camp until I have judged them completely with the weapons with which He has been defeating the enemy Satan for me throughout the course of history by sowing sweat for earth, tears for man, and blood for heaven as a servant but with a father's heart in order to restore His children and the universe, lost to Satan. This I pledge.

The individual, family, society, nation, world, and cosmos who are willing to attend our Father, the source of peace, happiness, freedom, and all ideals, will fulfill the ideal world of one heart in one body by restoring their original nature. To do this, I will become a true son [or daughter] returning joy and satisfaction to our Father, and as our Father's representative, I will transfer to the creation peace, happiness, freedom and all ideals in the world of the heart. This I pledge.

I am proud of the one Sovereignty, proud of the one people, proud of the one land, proud of the one language and culture centered upon God, proud of becoming the child of the One True Parent, proud of the family who is to inherit one tradition, proud of being a laborer who is working to establish the one world of the heart.

I will fight with my life.

I will be responsible for accomplishing my duty and mission.

This I pledge and swear.

"The final phrase, 'This I pledge and swear,' is repeated three times. It all sounds very ghostly at 5:00 A.M.

"Then there's a prayer led by the center director, and it's usually a pretty lengthy prayer — twenty minutes. At the conclusion of the service, everyone prays in unison, aloud. You rededicate your entire life and reassess your spiritual situation and set a tone for the coming week. Afterwards, you're told that you can go back to bed. But if you're a devoted member, you wouldn't think of going back to bed.

"We viewed prayer as if God had a bank account and Satan had a bank account and prayer consisted of payment. If the prayer was completely pure, then God would be able to accept it in His account. But if, for example, you prayed for four hours and then fell asleep during the last three minutes, your prayer was invalidated: then it went into Satan's bank account. You had to make up that prayer to get the books even again. You had to pray again in order to fill up God's bank account. The worst possible thing was to fall asleep during prayer. So you had to keep yourself awake; you had to hit yourself or poke yourself with pins. And if you had a close friend, they would help you every time you were going to fall asleep.

"You would really begin to believe that prayer was so powerful that just by your thought you could direct people to do whatever you wanted. For example, if you fasted for three days, to get a convert, you would become convinced that they couldn't resist. We would also have all-night prayer vigils and more extended periods of prayer or fasting with a specific goal in mind. These projects were called 'conditions' and were viewed as an offering to God. It could consist of prayer, fasting, or even cold showers. You always had to clear it with the person above you, your superior. If you did a condition on your own, it was not acceptable to God. Conditions had to be done for 3, 4, 7, 21, 40, or 120 days. You were not allowed to use any other numbers. If you did something for three days or if you had a condition for three days, then at the end of three days the spiritual conditions around you would change.

"We also had a specific ceremony for marking off and consecrating to God a particular spot of land. We called it 'holy ground.' Holy ground was supposedly land which had been reclaimed from Satan. The ceremony for making ground holy included taking earth from the original holy ground in Korea and burying it a prescribed number of feet under the ground. The end result was that you would feel immediately upon entering a particular area that this is where God dwells.

"There was also widespread use of 'holy salt.' Most Moonies carry holy salt with them at all times, in order to sanctify their food. Everything has to be sanctified before you eat. If you don't have holy salt to sanctify the food, you must blow on it three times. If you stay in a motel room with a fund-raising team, you have to sanctify the room first. You put three handfuls of holy salt in the middle of the room and then sprinkle salt around the room as you repeat a certain prayer. You have to open the windows and doors so the spirits can get out. If they are stupid spirits, they won't realize that they can go through the wall, and so they'll be looking for the door. You have to open the door in case they happen to be stupid spirits.

"If you were sick or in a bad mood, you would use holy salt. The spirits supposedly entered through the back of the neck, and you could sanctify yourself by getting them off the back of your neck. If someone freaked out, you would throw holy salt on them. I remember one evening my best girl friend experienced some kind of possession and started talking very strangely. So we threw holy salt on her and immediately felt the atmosphere in the room change. The spirits left, and she became normal.

"IN THE movement there was always a lot of talk about spirits and the spirit world. It wasn't anything unusual for me to see a spirit walk into a room and sit down and talk. There was also a tremendous emphasis on visions and personal revelation. It was considered a mark of distinction if you had visions. Many times when we stayed up late, we would see all kinds of things. I heard voices a lot and frequently hallucinated. I don't know why, perhaps from sleep deprivation. But it was a common experience, and it was encouraged. I saw a choir of angels once: they were singing in Korean. By the way, we were encouraged to learn Korean because eventually it would become the universal language. Even Jesus, of course, spoke Korean."

According to the theology of the Unification Church, Jesus was a sinless man but he failed in his mission. Ever since the fall of Adam and Eve, God has wanted to restore men to Himself through a spiritual and physical redemption. The Moonies teach that the crucifixion of Christ was a tragedy because it prevented him from finding the perfect mate and founding God's perfect family on earth, thus achieving both the physical and the spiritual salvation of man. Because Jesus saved man only spiritually, the Moonies teach that the messiah, or Lord of the Second Advent, must be born on earth in order to accomplish man's physical salvation. They teach that all religions will unite under this messiah.

For Shelley, the cross became a symbol of Satan's victory. "In Unification theology the cross actually becomes synonymous with Satan. I had been wearing a cross, and no way was I going to continue wearing it. We would comment, as we drove through a city, how ironic that all the churches had crosses on them, because the cross was a symbol of Satan.

"To a Moonie, 'Christian' is a bad word. Someone who's a Christian is immediately off limits when witnessing. A Christian is a person that you don't like. Moonies have a horror of Christians. They say their Bibles are like rifles and they come in and shoot Bible verses at you without really understanding the heart of the Bible. They say that Christians are the very ones who will crucify the new messiah. They're the enemy."

In a speech to his followers in October 1974, Reverend Moon spoke bluntly about Christian ministers and laymen who oppose him: "They are against me. . . . They are weak people. Those Christians are already out of the sight of God. God is leaving them, and they are destined to perish. The Christian world is now crumbling." Moon went on to ask the question, Are we going to build our movement stronger to win the fight against them?

Virtually all Moon's speeches to the faithful are transcribed and translated into English. They are circulated under the general title "Master Speaks" to leaders of the Unification Church throughout the United States. Occasionally excerpts are read to trainees during workshop programs, but they are never allowed to be seen by the public or by the new trainees. Shelley notes, "We were strictly warned about guarding them with our lives lest they fall into 'the hands of Satan.' They were considered as sacred to us as the Torah is to the Jews. We would hardly say a sentence without quoting them."

BECAUSE OF the drastic changes they saw taking place in their daughter, Shelley's parents felt they had to retrieve her from the cult. "I would have never left by myself," Shelley concedes. "I was firmly convinced that I was doing the right thing. I would have never left. They contrived a story and got me to leave the camp. It's a long story, but they finally got me out of there with the help of two friends on a dark night. They got me into a car, took me to a house in Long Beach where I was confined for three days, and deprogramed. Although I was locked up in a room, I was very comfortable; whatever I wanted they brought me.

"I don't think it would have worked if they had just tried to talk to me at a coffee shop or something. As long as it was on my own terms, we could have talked for days and they would have never made any headway. But as long as I knew that it was not on my terms, I had to think.

"I had a locket with Moon's picture in it, and on the first night of the deprograming, I very quietly slid the picture out of the locket and swallowed it. I didn't want anything done to that photograph: I was deathly afraid that they would put a mustache or something on it. For about a month after leaving the movement, I still couldn't look at a picture of Moon. I just couldn't stand to look at him, because I had loved him so much."

There were other problems during those first few weeks out of the cult. Shelley's cognitive processes were scrambled. "Every time I would try to think, it was like touching the wrong buzzer, and the sound would go off in my head, but I couldn't think. It was like all those communication circuits in my brain were just fractured. And I haven't cried since I've been out. I'm a very emotional person, and I always cried while in the movement. I still have nightmares every night, but it's wonderful to be able to wake up in the morning and say, 'Thank God, I can do what I want today.'"

◆ SIX ◆

The Way

MARIE LEONETTI grew up in the Detroit area and attended Catholic schools through senior high. After graduation, she enrolled in a suburban community college with her future plans still uncertain.

"I was into my second year and had no real direction. I was just going because it seemed the thing to do. I was depressed because I had to decide what I was going to do with myself and my college education. I was depressed about the friends I was hanging around with: I didn't particularly care for them. In other words, I was depressed about a lot of things.

"One day while I was in the student union, I met some nice, smiling people who said they were having Bible fellowships in their homes in the evenings. Because I was raised a Catholic, I didn't get too much Bible teaching, and that was one thing I was hungry for. They told me they were just Christians who read and studied the Bible together. They said they weren't a church and they weren't a religious denomination. And so I thought, 'Fine. This is really nice; it's not going to detract from my religion, it's just something to add to it.' They had also mentioned a class called 'Power for Abundant Living' that I could take if I wanted to.

"That first night I went, I found the people to be smiling and friendly and warm. They said things like 'We love you' and 'God bless you.' I had never associated with people who had said things like that so freely. I really liked it, so I came back again and decided to go once a week. About a week later they mentioned the class again. I thought to myself, 'I really don't need to take a Bible class; I'll just go to the fellowship once a week.'

The next time I went, we were sitting around talking after the Bible study and they handed me a green card. It turned out to be the registration card for the Power for Abundant Living class. I really didn't want to sign up for the class, but everyone there had taken it or at least were in the process of taking it. They were such nice people and they were nice new friends, so I decided to take the class."

The course in which Marie enrolled, billed by its promoters as "The most amazing class in the world," consisted of listening to thirty-three hours of tapes over a three-week period. In any given week it is estimated that one thousand Americans are pursuing "the more than abundant life" at a cost of $85 — the "minimum required donation." The poster advertising the class promises, "YOU CAN HAVE WHATEVER YOU WANT! Every problem you ever had can be overcome when you are fully and accurately instructed."

"I really couldn't afford the eighty-five dollars, since I wasn't making much money at the time. I was going to school and only working one or two days a week, so I didn't make much more than eighty-five dollars over a period of two weeks. They said, 'God can meet your needs, believe Him to supply you with the money.' I didn't know what they were talking about. But I believed them and gave them the eighty-five dollars for the class."

THE POWER for Abundant Living course (PFAL) was developed by The Way International, a Bible research and teaching organization with headquarters in New Knoxville, Ohio. The founder, president, and prophet of The Way is Victor Paul Wierwille, 59, a former minister of the Evangelical and Reformed Church. Wierwille holds a master's degree from Princeton Seminary and was awarded the doctor of theology degree from Pike's Peak Theological Seminary, an alleged degree mill, in 1948. For a number of years "Doctor" Wierwille (as he is affectionately called by his followers) served in a pastorate in northwestern Ohio. During this time he searched the Bible for "keys to powerful victorious living" and in 1953 began teaching the class on Power for Abundant Living. He is a self-proclaimed Greek and Hebrew scholar who has written a number of books and pamphlets, published by his own organization. His movement has an estimated twenty thousand followers found in all fifty states and thirty-seven foreign countries. The Way magazine has a circulation of over ten thousand and is also distributed from the international headquarters, Wierville's family farm near New Knoxville, Ohio.

In the fall of 1974, Wierwille acquired the forty-one-acre campus of a Presbyterian college in Emporia, Kansas, forced to close because of financial difficulties. Now known as The Way College of Emporia, it has a student body of over four hundred and offers a curriculum of biblical studies "found nowhere else in our country."

No doubt related to this bold assertion is the fact that Wierwille claims to have received direct audible communication from God. "He said He would teach me the Word as it had not been known since the first century if I would teach it to others," Wierwille recalls. This promise, plus Wierwille's purported thirty-four years of Bible study and research, allows adherents of The Way to conclude that they have a corner on the Truth. As Marie was told, "Sure people were Christians all along, but no one had the real Truth like we have the real Truth."

Marie learned during her PFAL class that Wierwille claims to have rediscovered the long lost "true" teachings of the original apostles. "When everyone gets out of this class, they believe that, because he's convinced them. Dr. Wierwille is said to be the greatest teacher since the apostle Paul. It is an unwritten fact that Dr. Wierwille is believed to be an apostle. They believe that they constitute the true body of believers because they have more truth than anyone else.

"During the first class session, the introductory tape instructed us to 'just sit back and listen.' For the entire three weeks of class, you can't ask any questions and you cannot take any notes. You sit there and listen and look at your Bible: that's all you can do. Then, at the conclusion of the three-week course, if you should happen to remember some of the questions that you had, you have to write them down on a piece of paper and give them in before your last session. They really don't make that clear, however. Before the last session started, they said, 'Do you have your questions to hand in?' I didn't know we were supposed to have them written down, so I didn't get to hand in any questions. We were also not allowed to ask questions during the regular fellowship and Bible study sessions. If you had a question then, you would be taken off to the side afterwards so that you wouldn't influence any other new people there.

"In session 12 of the Power for Abundant Living class, you get a surprise: they teach you how to speak in tongues. If questioned on this matter, they will say, 'We don't teach anyone; we lead them into it.' They're very careful with their words. But they really do teach you, and you learn by observation. Typically, you attend a lot of fellowships before you take the PFAL class, and so you hear people speaking in tongues many times. You keep going to fellowships all along, and you hear it, and they tell you. 'Everyone is different. Yours isn't going to sound like someone else's.' So when you get to session 12, whatever you blurt out is okay. It doesn't matter what word you're saying, as long as you're just blurting out these meaningless words. It's very much like when you're a child in kindergarten learning a song: all you have to do is hear it enough times and you know all the words, you know all the notes.

"We were told to S.I.T. [speak in tongues] as much as possible during the day. You do it automatically, because you don't have to think about it. Once you learn how to do it, it's just a bunch of babbling. Some Way children also speak in tongues as soon as they are old enough to talk. I personally knew of two young boys, aged three and four, who had been taught to speak in tongues." In *Receiving the Holy Spirit Today*, Wierwille prescribes the procedure to follow in order to speak in tongues. The book is described as a "how-to-do-it book" by Wierwille himself, and he outlines the four steps leading up to the tongues experience. First, one must become quiet and relaxed. Second, the seeker need not beg God for the experience. Third, "rest your head back and breathe in deeply.... By believing, you can breathe in the spirit. Opening your mouth and breathing in deeply is an act of believing which God honors" (p. 60). Finally, Wierwille suggests the following prayer: "Father, I now receive the holy spirit, the power from on high, which you made available through Jesus Christ." He continues,

> Having carried out these four simple steps to receiving the power of the holy spirit, you must now by your own will, move your lips, your tongue, your throat; you must make the sounds, form the words. . . . What you speak is God's business; but that you speak is your business (p. 62).

Note that in the quoted passage, Wierwille uses a small h and a small s in discussing an impersonal "holy spirit," a gift, as opposed to "the Holy Spirit," the Giver. Wierwille believes that the Holy Spirit is the Father [God] by another name and that the holy spirit is merely "power from on high." In short, Wierwille rejects the Person of the Holy Spirit.

ONE OF Wierwille's most recent books is entitled *Jesus Christ is NOT God.* It underscores Wierwille's basic theological precept that God is one in substance and only one in Person. He teaches that Jesus and God are not the same; that Jesus was specially created by God in Mary's womb, a perfect man, but not God. Therefore, according to The Way, it is acceptable to call Jesus the Son of God, but not God the Son.

Not only does Wierwille totally deny the doctrine of the Trinity, but he also rejects the Old Testament as having any validity for Christians: only the New Testament epistles apply to believers today. Wierwille teaches that Christ was crucified on Wednesday, not on Friday; that four thieves were crucified with Christ, not two; that Jesus was not a Jew, but "a Judean"; and that human beings experience a kind of "soul sleep" upon death.

Marie soon discovered that there was a series of PFAL classes — she had completed merely the foundational class. That is followed by an "Intermediate" class which in turn is followed by an "Advanced" class. None is free. "I continued going to fellowships in private homes, and after about three months I was ready for the Intermediate class. Here they teach you to interpret tongues and to prophesy. It was all built on the foundational class. Now I could speak in tongues, interpret, and prophesy, which amounted to no more than repeating things I had heard in the fellowship groups."

Despite her parents' warnings and concern, Marie was increasingly coming under the influence of The Way. "One day someone from the state headquarters in Michigan came to talk to me personally. I was very impressed — why would he want to talk with me? We went for a nice long walk and talked about how corrupt the world was becoming and how much badness there was because of Satan's activity. He said that the only thing that's going to save the world is God's Word. At the end of this conversation, he turned to me and said, 'Now Marie, the best thing you can do in this situation — the very best thing for you to do — is to go out as a WOW Ambassador.' WOW stands for Word over the World. As a WOW Ambassador, you go to another part of the United States for a year and witness to people and get them to take the PFAL class.

"I told him I was ready to go. This was in June, and I soon learned that I was scheduled to leave at the end of August. Somehow I had to tell my parents that I would be gone for a year. The problem was, I didn't know where I was going, because they never assigned you until the night before you actually left. I finally told my parents, and naturally, they didn't want me to go."

Marie was sent to Texas for a year to fulfill the stated objective of a WOW Ambassador: "to open and establish areas in the accuracy of God's Word." What this really amounts to is establishing local fellowships and running Power for Abundant Living courses. According to the WOW Handbook, ambassadors must put in a minimum of eight hours a day in Way-related witnessing. In addition, they must obtain part-time jobs (a minimum of twenty hours per week, maximum thirty) in order to support themselves. Marie held a series of part-time jobs and turned 15 to 20 percent of her income over to The Way (a tithe of 10 percent is considered the minimum one owes God, according to Wierwille's teaching). She lived with her spiritual family (two boys and another girl), and their combined part-time salaries paid for the rent, food, and other expenses. Together they constituted the local fellowship group, the hub of the organization's witnessing outreach.

THE WAY'S organizational structure is described in terms of a tree analogy. The smallest local unit is known as a Twig fellowship. Several household fellowship groups make up a Branch, or city unit. Each statewide unit is a Limb. Limb leaders report to Regional Directors, who funnel information back to the International Coordinator in Ohio, where the organizational tree is firmly rooted in Wierwille's family homestead.

In Texas, Marie took a class in witnessing and undershepherding. The witnessing objective of WOW Ambassadors is "Each one win one." There was great emphasis on door-to-door witnessing. Members are told to read Dale Carnegie's book, *How to Win Friends and Influence People,* and to apply its principles to witnessing. They are told not to argue. The WOW Handbook states,

> Since truth needs no defense, we should develop a strong offense in challenging those who propound error. An effective strategy is to answer a question with a question. This shifts the burden of proof to the person who refutes the truth.

Marie and her friends witnessed in stores, restaurants, and other public places. They were taught to look for young people who appeared lonely, unhappy, or confused. Undershepherds were instructed to show the potential convert that he was loved: "Do little things for him; let him know that you are willing to help him whenever he needs it (even at 3:00 A.M.). Be a faithful shepherd, see your person every day."

As a WOW Ambassador, Marie was encouraged to enroll in The Way Corps, a three-year leadership training program conducted in Kansas. "If I wanted to be a great leader, if I wanted to really lead God's people, the best thing for me to do was to go into The Way Corps for three years. The cost is $300 a month, and you are not permitted to hold a job while in training." Way Corps applicants must obtain their own funding by lining up a series of "sponsors," individuals willing to make regular, monthly financial commitments in support of Corps members. Applicants to The Way Corps are encouraged to write letters to prospective sponsors, suggesting that they contribute $5, $10, or $15 per month.

Marie decided to enter the leadership training program

because of her basic desire to help people. "I really wanted to help people with God's Word. But first you have to learn it, you have to learn the accuracy of God's Word. So in order to help even more, I went into The Way Corps.

"My parents weren't very pleased about my going to Emporia. At that time they still didn't realize that I was a member of a cult. Although they disagreed with the organization, they really didn't have enough information at that point to evaluate it. They concluded that since they couldn't stop me from going to Texas, they wouldn't be able to stop me from going to Kansas either. And they were right — nothing could have stopped me. By that time, I had lost my free will. I no longer was doing the things I wanted to do. I was programed into the group; I was just a little Way robot."

A WAY CORPS member's life is rigidly structured and scheduled. Each person is required to keep a daily, hour-by-hour record of how he spends his time. The form, called a "Redeemed Time Analysis," contains a column headed "How I Spent My Time" and another column, "How I Can Improve." There is space for entries opposite every hour beginning with 5:00 A.M. and ending with midnight. "These are the people who are going to be their leaders, and they want them right there, right at the end of their little finger," Marie notes. "That's why everyone eats the same, that's why everybody brushes their teeth the same way.

"When we went into the Way Corps, we were told to bring a diary with us. We were expected to keep up our diaries and to keep them positive. They didn't want you to be negative or to think badly of yourself at all. They wanted to keep building your ego."

Another apparent objective of the Way Corps program is to build physically fit leaders. Regular daily exercise is required. "The first month or so that I was there I didn't do my exercises regularly at all. I'd do them maybe three times a week. When they found out that people weren't faithfully doing their exercises, the leaders felt they were losing a measure of control. After a while we had to mark down on a chart every day that we'd completed our exercises and list the specific exercises that we did, making sure we did every single exercise. In actuality, their idea of total fitness is much more mental fitness: they want to toughen their people up mentally.

"One of our classes started right after supper, and it was difficult to get there on time. It was the instructor's policy that if you were not there ten minutes early, you would be considered late. People were regularly coming in right before class started, and so they were considered late. One night after the class was dismissed, the instructor decided to discipline us for being late. We were told to go to our rooms, put on our sweatsuits, and return to a designated place in twenty minutes. First, we had to go through our entire physical fitness routine that we had already completed earlier in the day. It takes about forty-five minutes to complete, including calisthenics, rope-climbing, pull-ups, and running. He told us, 'Run further than you've ever run before.' Some people were running three miles every day, so they had to run more than three miles. When we completed our running, we all did calisthenics together. Then we did some very difficult routines that are sometimes done in football drills: we had to hit the ground and then jump up right away.

"It was after 10:00 P.M. and I started crying — I was so upset. I was physically exhausted, and I was mentally hurt. When we were all done, the instructor said, 'If you want to get extra blessing, run around the track a couple of times.' I was so tired, but I did it! All of this was punishment for coming late to class: 'You're not on time if you're not there ten minutes early.'

"I remember going back to my room and crying. I thought, *Why are they making us do this?* I concluded to myself, *It's just discipline — I've got to be disciplined; I've got to be able to handle this type of situation.* . . . I remembered someone saying, 'There may come a time when we have to go underground — you never know. So we've got to be able to handle this.'"

The meals at The Way Corps were insubstantial. "Everyone lost weight. And you never got enough sleep. I got maybe four or five hours every night. It's a pretty rigorous schedule there. The day starts at 5:00 A.M. when you get up and either study or do your exercises. Usually you had a very physical job for half of the day. And then you studied the other half. Then you're up late at night listening to lecture classes. If you happen to start to doze, you're quickly nudged or someone will put their hand on your back to wake you up. They don't want you to get ripped off of the blessing of the lecture."

For backpacking and mountaineering enthusiasts, the Power for Abundant Living class is also offered as an integral part of the Total Fitness Institute, a wilderness survival program located in the California Sierras. The director spent five years as an instructor at the Marine Corps Physical Fitness Academy and served as an assistant football coach at Princeton and Ohio State. The program cost is $275 for two weeks.

Members of The Way Corps who wanted to attend TFI had to hitchhike there. "They send them with twenty dollars for expenses and they must come back with twenty. They have to make the money along the way. Wierwille wants his people to be mentally and physically strong."

LIKE MOST cult groups, Wierwille's Way offers considerable security. "You don't have to make any decisions. You don't have to worry about the future, because The Way has made all your plans for you. There's always someone in the group to correct you, to take away your doubts, your worries."

With security, there is often control. Marie discovered that the group's control extended to everyday necessities: "They explained, 'It's not love to use too much toilet paper.' We were made to feel bad for using too much toilet paper."

But another form of control is also characteristic of closed systems. This form of control is far more frightening in its implications — mind control. Marie feels that gradually, over a period of time, she became the victim of a subtle form of mind manipulation. She describes the results: "Your mind is always geared and directed. You no longer think for yourself. You think what you're told to think. What I experienced when I came out was that it was hard to think; it was hard to put my thoughts together in order to say anything. And sometimes now, I still stumble for words or stumble over how to put something together. It's like my mind was asleep for a while. It's a real subtle kind of control over the mind, and no one ever feels it coming over them."

MARIE WAS a member of The Way for twenty-two months. "While I was in it, I never would have come out on my own, because I had found the Truth. Nothing that anyone could say, nothing that I could read, nothing that I could think would have convinced me otherwise. We were told that Satan would stop at nothing to get us away from the truth. They said, 'Satan will work through your parents and try to get you away from the Truth.' So naturally, when my parents or friends started questioning me about my involvement with The Way, I knew that Satan was using them. Nothing they could say could change my mind."

During the fall of Marie's last year with The Way, her parents obtained additional information about the organization and concluded that it was cultic. "When my parents found out what was really going on, they intended to rescue me from it. When I came home for Christmas, they wouldn't let me go back. They had some people talk to me, and after three and a half days I was deprogramed. During this process, I started using my mind once again, thinking for myself, starting to make decisions once again. That was the greatest thing that ever happened to me."

The Way International celebrated its thirty-fifth anniversary in 1977. Victor Paul Wierwille continues to proclaim what he believes to be the only true, accurate interpretation of God's Word. He still blasts away at Billy Graham and at the institutional church, recently charging that deprograming is financed by the denominations. His choicest words of wrath are reserved for the Living Bible, which he considers to be no more than a "bunch of junk." As Wierwille sees it, "The devil himself couldn't have written it any better." And as far as he is concerned, those responsible for introducing it to Americans ". . . ought to be in jail — they ought to be incarcerated for ninety-nine years."

Way followers continue to peddle the abundant life — at a modest fee. They have set a goal of six thousand College Ambassadors to "open up" all the major campuses in the nation. With an eye to young people like Marie, they have concluded, "This gives us great access to the future leaders of the world."

◆ SEVEN ◆

The Divine Light Mission

JIM ARDMORE was a twenty-five-year-old social worker employed by the State of Michigan at the time he was introduced to the Divine Light Mission. A well-read and highly articulate graduate of Michigan State University, Jim was acquainted with the literature then popular with many young people in the university subculture — the writing of Dr. Richard Alpert, and Carlos Castenada's books about Yaqui Indian sorcery. Books such as these, with a clear countercultural flavor, presented the model of a spiritual teacher imparting specialized and mysterious spiritual knowledge to his followers. Jim had also developed an interest in Transcendental Meditation as a result of his association with some friends who had been meditating for several years.

"I got promoted into a job where I was really in over my head. The new position involved finding jobs for people who didn't want to work. It was a pretty frustrating, depressing job. One day I received a letter from a young man inviting me to come to a meeting and learn about Guru Maharaj Ji, the fifteen-year-old Perfect Master from India. The invitation stated that I would learn four techniques of meditation completely free of charge. These included seeing Divine Light, hearing the music of the spheres [Divine Music] with the inner ear, tasting Nectar, and perceiving the Word [Holy Name of God] within oneself.

"I was a little suspicious about all this, so I went and asked a friend of mine who was knowledgeable about Eastern religion: 'What do you know about this guru?' He replied that he had heard nothing bad about the guru and that some of his devotees seemed to be happy, loving people. So I decided to check it out. I went to a public meeting on the Michigan State campus the following week. At the entrance to the auditorium, there was a literature table where some friendly people suggested that I go in and sit down, which I did. I was feeling a little bit awkward with my long hair and my beard in the midst of a group of clean-shaven young men with short hair, wearing coats and ties. And they all had very shining-looking faces.

"By the time the program started, the auditorium was packed. The person who was supposed to speak was the guru's disciple, Mahatma Parlokanand. But first a Hawaiian fellow came up on the stage and started playing the guitar and leading singing. The first song they sang was 'Amazing Grace,' with particular emphasis on the line, 'When we've been there ten thousand years, bright shining as the sun. . . .' The references to light and sound in the songs were especially appropriate to their purpose. At the time it just struck me as being corny. They sang a song which proclaimed, 'Lord of the Universe, come to us this day. Open up your hearts to the Universe of Love, and He will fill you up.' Everybody there was young; everybody was either serene or ecstatic or very, very loving.

"Finally the mahatma came in, prostrated himself in front of the guru's picture, sat down, and sang a quotation from Shankara. He started telling parables which sounded like Indian folk tales: they were about kings and beggars and thieves and elephants and pools and birds and necklaces. Perfect spiritual knowledge was being offered at absolute discount — completely free.

"They gave an address where we could go to get more information. Then more songs were sung. People got up and talked about how miserable they were before they received the perfect spiritual knowledge and how everything was perfectly happy now. The meeting ended and we left."

AT THIS juncture in Jim's life, he was not particularly religiously oriented. "I had been vaguely Christian before I entered college. Until I was in the fourth grade, we attended a nondenominational church, and then we switched to a Methodist church because my father liked the minister. Throughout high school we attended a Presbyterian church. I sang in the choir and spent a couple of summers at Westminister Choir College Vocal Camp. Then I went to college and lived in an environment where nobody went to church.

"I went to the address I had been given and knocked on the door. There was no answer. Finally I opened the door, walked in, and was greeted by a sign: HOME IS WHERE THE HEART IS. NO SMOKING. PLEASE REMOVE YOUR SHOES. There was a pile of shoes inside the door, so I took off mine. I entered a rather sparsely furnished living room which contained a little altar. I recognized the guru's picture. I heard somebody playing the guitar upstairs, so I went up and introduced myself to a young man who had obviously been meditating while playing his guitar. As I walked toward him, he opened his eyes and I said, 'I want to learn how to meditate.' He replied by saying something like 'Our generation has really been looking for this for a long time. We looked for it in peace politics, in street politics, in drugs and underground newspapers.' He hadn't gone much further before I was getting extraordinarily bored. I didn't want to listen to what our generation had been going through: I knew. I wanted to learn how to meditate. And he didn't look very spiritual — he was too healthy looking. After a few minutes, in came the guy who had written me the letter, Mark. He was a guy who looked like a true spiritual seeker: he was skinny; he was very cheerful, very happy, very open. He looked right at me, right into my eyes, and said, 'This is it. This is what you've been looking for.'

"I had the feeling that he was being completely honest with me. I just wanted to learn how to meditate, and he again said that it was completely free. 'All you have to do is ask for it.' But he said that he couldn't teach me. I'd have to learn from Mahatma."

IN THE Divine Light Mission, the ultimate spiritual experience is receiving "the Knowledge." Knowledge is given by Guru Maharaj Ji, "the Perfect Master of our time," who dispenses it to sincere seekers via a few special disciples called mahatmas.

The guru explains why one should "take Knowledge": "You will be in perfection. Then you will be guided by God. Perfect guidance will be given to you. So just realize the perfect aim of your life, why you have come into this world."

There are only a few mahatmas in all North America who give Knowledge, so the would-be "premies" (devotees) must follow them around from city to city until they are finally admitted to a "Knowledge session." Prior to this, it is important that the new recruits listen to *satsang*, spiritual discourses. An introductory *satsang* is usually available at the local ashram, or temple, for those persons interested in finding out more about the Knowledge. Once *satsang* has been heard and there is a serious interest in receiving Knowledge, the aspirants are encouraged to attend a weekly *satsang*.

Jim was told that the mahatma was in another city, and he was encouraged to seek him out. "If you're really sincere, you can go right now. He doesn't take everybody right away. He has to believe that you're really sincere. He has to see you out a little while. Maybe you should go there today — you should go there tonight." Jim protested: "I have to go to work tomorrow." The reply was, "Just call your supervisor; it'll be okay."

Hesitantly Jim called his supervisor and asked for a day off for "personal business." Jim was astonished when his boss agreed because of the workload at the office. "I concluded, 'Obviously I'm supposed to be doing this.' I was starting to get into their frame of mind already."

It was the middle of January, and it was snowing. Jim drove to another city in search of the mahatma only to learn that the Hindu apostle had already selected fifteen people for admission to the Knowledge session. Jim wasn't discouraged. "I really wanted the perfect spiritual knowledge, since everybody was talking it up so much." Along with a group of other aspirants, he listened to *satsang* over the weekend and returned to his job Monday. He asked for time off to follow the mahatma around, but it was denied. One day he decided to take a week off anyway and drove to Chicago in search of the Knowledge.

A few days before the next scheduled Knowledge session, the mahatma had said to the devotees, "Give your love to Guru Maharaj Ji, and he will give you the Perfect Knowledge." At the time, Jim was feeling pretty depressed: "I'd been feeling like I was not loving enough, and I was depressed for various reasons. I'd been married for about two years and was divorced in the previous spring. I was going through a whole lot of stuff. It was a very bad year for me. And then the job.

"I was admitted to the Knowledge session on the twenty-sixth of February at three in the morning. As we prepared for the Knowledge session, we were told we should concentrate on how much we wanted the perfect spiritual knowledge. We were not to let our minds wander. In my mind I was singing a devotional song which went like this: 'I love you my Lord, your grace is overflowing; I love you my Lord, you are all-knowing. You have given me life out of your mercy and compassion. I am so grateful for the gift of devotion.'

"All fifteen of us were seated in a darkened room when all of a sudden the mahatma came in, sat down, and turned on the only light in the room. Just as he entered the room I felt this strange force inside my head. I felt as if I were blasted by some kind of energy coming from somewhere in the direction of the mahatma. I was just loaded with love. It was just pure love, really strong. And it kept getting stronger, more intense. I was feeling like a rickety-framed house about to collapse in a wind storm. *I won't be able to take it*, I thought. Tears were streaming down my cheeks. The emotion was just flowing. I hadn't cried since I was in the first grade.

"Then the mahatma began to talk about the light. He said, 'The light will purify you if you meditate on it, but you will not see the light if your mind is active.'

"Then he indicated that we should concentrate on the groove in our eyebrow ridge just above the nose. We put our index finger on the groove — that was the place where we were to concentrate. We were not to turn our eyes upward. Then he said he would give us the Knowledge. He would touch us on the forehead and we would see the Light. He turned off the one light in the room and began walking in the dark. I was sitting there with my eyes closed, waiting. Suddenly I felt him swishing by, and I could feel his finger on my forehead. Then all of a sudden, I felt his fingers on my eyes. Instantly I was zapped with light and was seeing a figure eight of pure white light. It was brilliant, dazzling. Then the mahatma took my right hand and put my index finger against my forehead, my thumb and my middle finger against my eyes. My left hand supported my right elbow, and in that position he left me. After he had initiated everybody, he told us to meditate for one hour, and then he left the room.

"When he returned, we went through a ritual that was to enable us to hear Divine Music. We were to concentrate on whatever we heard on the right side of our head. What we heard on the left side was evil, the left side was of the body — mortal; the right side was immortal. All I could hear was a ringing sound. After an hour, the mahatma returned to teach us the Word, the Holy Name of God. We learned to pronounce the name through a series of deep breathing exercises. It involved the sound of our own breathing.

"The mahatma returned one final time so that we could learn about the Nectar. We were told to turn our tongues back and that our tongues would naturally find the passageway to where the Nectar drips down. I didn't taste anything. Nobody tasted anything except one guy over in the corner who exclaimed how everything smelled like roses and how sweet everything was.

"At this point the mahatma got down on his knees, turned around to an altar, and asked us to repeat after him: 'I promise that I will always implicitly obey the commandments of Guru Maharaj Ji.' He said, 'Now you may do whatever you want, but make sure you meditate while you're doing it. Meditation will act as a sail on a sailboat and will always bring you back to Guru Maharaj Ji.'

The mahatma said the best way to live is with other devotees, to share everything except our clothing. 'You should not share your clothing, because you will pick up each other's vibrations. You should not eat meat, because it's impure — you pick up meat vibrations. You should not wear long hair, because this is impurity. You don't carry your excreta around in paper bags; same manner, you should not have long hair. This is impurity.'

"He concluded: 'Go now, the general secretary will give you an envelope. You should go back to whatever you do.'

"It had been over a week since I was on the job. After I had been gone for two days, they had sent me a registered letter stating that if I didn't come back within two weeks I would be considered to have resigned. I went back before the two weeks was up, and I worked a couple of days. I was just higher than a kite: I was God talking to God, standing on God, breathing God. My supervisor was angry; he wanted me to resign. Obviously anybody who went off chasing after some guru could not be considered very reliable.

"I really wanted to resign anyway. I decided that I couldn't be a welfare worker while going around trying to convert everybody; I was trying to serve two masters. That wasn't appropriate, so I resigned."

HAVING EXPERIENCED the initiation ceremony of receiving Knowledge, Jim was now a member of a world-wide organization, the Divine Light Mission (DLM). The teen-age Indian guru who heads the movement is reported to have six million Indian devotees and over fifty thousand followers in the West. His father, Shri Hans Maharaj Ji, spent his life spreading the basic ideas of DLM throughout India and West Pakistan. His wife, Mata Ji, bore him four sons, the youngest being Guru Maharaj Ji. In 1966, when the guru was eight years old, his father died, and he assumed leadership of the movement. This took place in dramatic fashion, as reported by the monthly DLM magazine, *And It Is Divine*:

> On August 1, 1966, Guru Maharaj Ji stood up in front of the thousands of devotees present at His father's funeral to speak: "Dear Children of God, why are you weeping? Haven't you learned the lesson that your Master taught you? The Perfect Master never dies. Maharaj Ji is here, amongst you now. Recognize Him, obey Him, and worship Him" (*November 1972*).

Guru Maharaj Ji is considered by his devotees to be a *satguru*, or Perfect Master. In Hindi *sat* means truth, *gu* means darkness, and *ru* means light. A guru is therefore one who leads from darkness to light. Guru Maharaj Ji teaches his followers how to become perfect by "giving Knowledge" and by instructing them to meditate upon it. This Knowledge is said to be an intangible essence or energy which involves a direct experience of God. The Knowledge emanates from Guru Maharaj Ji but is transferred to initiates through specially designated disciples of the guru, called mahatmas.

After receiving the Knowledge, the new premie (devotee) is advised to meditate upon the Light, Music, Nectar, and Word for at least two hours a day. To achieve spiritual advancement, Guru Maharaj Ji recommends that a premie's life be devoted to four primary activities: meditation, darshan (physical sight of the Guru), satsang (spiritual discourse), and service. Of these four, meditation is the most significant. The premie is told to meditate continually on the Word; it becomes the primary objective and duty of the devotee. As Jim put it, "The mind had to be controlled. The mind was controlled by meditation."

The commandment to meditate continually may result in extraordinary consequences. Jim reports that some of his acquaintances in the movement literally lost the ability to read. "People around me were saying things like 'Wow, how can you still read?' They said if they meditate, they couldn't read. I myself lost the ability to add and subtract. I could not balance a checkbook. I was always spaced out. At this point, I would accept almost anything my leaders told me, since I was not capable of questioning anything.

"I was asked one day whether I would die for the Guru Maharaj Ji, and when I replied that I would, I was told that I was making progress quickly. In fact, if the guru had instructed me to murder my mother at that time, I would have done so without hesitation, confident that I was doing her a favor."

The experience of darshan involves being in the physical presence of Guru Maharaj Ji. Whenever the opportunity presents itself, the devotee is expected to make some effort to be as physically close to the guru as possible. And since there is a spiritual polarity in the human body with a positive end and a negative end, it is hoped that the devotee will be able to kiss the guru's feet. When the follower does this for the first time, it also involves what is called "receiving the holy breath." According to Jim, "You're supposed to indicate your right ear, and he will blow into your right ear, and this will benefit your meditation and improve you spiritually."

Devotees who look at Maharaj Ji report seeing nothing but intense light. Some experience a complete stopping of time. Others find in his every motion, gesture, and word the answers to their most troubling questions and doubts. One devotee stated that she shivered in the cold for four hours waiting for the guru to deliver a five-minute speech. "In that time, fatigue, cold, hunger, uncertainty, irritation all vanished, and I felt fantastically energized, happy, and lighthearted." Others have related feelings of inexplicable happiness, a sense of floating in intense joy.

JIM HAD an opportunity to approach the "lotus feet" of the guru while in London during the summer of 1973. "After standing in line for six hours, I got within striking distance. But I didn't get close enough to kiss his feet. I got shoved by too fast, so all I could do was bend down and indicate my ear. I was expecting some kind of cosmic blast, and all that happened was a sense of something bubbling up from inside my mind."

Another method of receiving *darshan* is to *pranam*, or prostrate oneself on the ground in front of the guru without touching his feet. This prostration is symbolic of the devotee's complete surrender to the "greater reality." A DLM follower explains the experience:

One feels totally energized and full of life and one's consciousness becomes so pure and so intense that the experience is often described as stronger than LSD or other hallucinatory drugs. One's mind is instantly cleared; one's thoughts of the past and future and the condition of one's body drop away. One is left experiencing the moment directly as it is. One becomes totally calm and detached from everything and yet at the same time incredibly filled with energy and able to do nearly anything. Other people all seem beautiful and perfect, there is nothing to do but to hug them, one begins to feel a sense of infinite love for everyone and everything. One becomes irrationally happy without having taken any drugs.

Satsang is a kind of spiritual shot in the arm for DLM devotees. According to the guru, without *satsang* a premie really cannot thrive. He describes the importance of the practice in a message reprinted in the May 1976 issue of *Love Song*, a newsletter distributed by DLM of Los Angeles:

> Satsang is something which is very, very direct, *from* Guru Maharj Ji, *from* the doctor, to you. It's a direct cure; not just prescribing your medicine, a *more* direct thing. Premies come, sit down, and Guru Maharaj Ji comes and gives satsang, maybe they are just the nurses, or the assistant, but they can help you too. . . . That is why satsang is so important — to keep our mind where it *should* be, so that it's not affecting us the way it usually does.

The other activity comprising the ideal devotee's life is service. In its broadest sense, service is viewed as any physical or mental activity that is dedicated to Guru Maharaj Ji. Service is the "action" dimension of spiritual activity. Although "serving others" and "selfless service" are part of the official rhetoric, the average premie frequently experiences service by seeking donations, spreading information about DLM, or by participating in DUO — Divine United Organizations. DUO consists of a series of satellite operations including Shri Hans Productions, which publishes the newspaper *Divine Times* and the magazine *And It Is Divine* and produces films. DLM's equivalent to the Salvation Army's thrift stores are known as Divine Sales second-hand stores. There's also a Divine Clinic, drug rehabilitation centers, coffee shops, and restaurants.

THE DLM organization in the United States operates a chain of more than thirty ashrams. An ashram is where premies live and work. It serves as a center for DLM activity in a given locality. Each ashram is directed by a general secretary, who reports to headquarters in Denver, Colorado.

The organization pays no taxes on its reported monthly revenues of $355,000. According to DLM executive Bob Mischler, "We are a religion only through legal structures. What we really want to do is further human liberty."

If nothing else, the movement has clearly furthered the financial status of its teen-age leader. The guru smiles all the way to the bank in his $50,000 refrigerator-equipped Rolls Royce. The plump Perfect Master chews gum, loves ice cream, enjoys sports cars and cabin cruisers, and maintains a home in Denver and an estate at Malibu, California. His affluent life style, which hardly befits the ideal of traditional Indian gurus, caused a family feud when his mother, charging that Maharaj Ji had become a playboy, named her oldest son to replace his brother as new guru of the Divine Light Mission. The family battle caused a financial crisis and contributed to a drop in membership.

One source of income for the group is the donated gifts and possessions of new members. In one widely publicized case, a wealthy young heiress was willing to sign over an estimated $400,000 inheritance to the Divine Light Mission. As Jim describes it, "Service to humanity means giving money to the guru. You have to give up all your worldly possessions. When they heard that I had a trust fund, they said, "You should get that for the guru.' Because my mother was the trustee, they wanted me to convert her. I really couldn't move into the ashram unless I got that money and gave it to the guru."

An ashram is a kind of coed monastery where renunciant premies live and work. All residents are expected to observe ashram discipline, which includes (1) turning over all material possessions and earnings to the Divine Light Mission; (2) devoting all one's time to service; (3) obedience to the general secretary of the ashram, who determines service assignments, gives permission to come and go, and makes other decisions pertaining to the daily operation of the local organization; and (4) following the daily schedule, which usually allows only five hours of sleep and begins at five in the morning; (5) abstaining from alcohol, drugs, tobacco, meat, sex, and food not provided by the ashram.

Only a small proportion of American devotees live in ashrams and adhere to the discipline required of ashram life. Many premies who, after receiving Knowledge, do not feel they can submit to the rigor of the ashram, live together in "premie houses." These houses serve as information centers in communities where there are no ashrams, as homes for those involved in DLM activities, or simply as residences where premies can meditate together and provide each other with spiritual support.

Most devotees, whether living in a premie house or in an ashram, abstain from sexual activity, Jim reports. "Nobody was having sex. Some of the literature said that the guru expected that if you were having sex you would be married, and there was a kind of Roman Catholic morality about that. Sex was for the purpose of procreation; anything else was considered an 'attachment.' Birth control was something that you did because you were attached to sex and didn't want to have children. There were always a few people around, with a certain kind of ego, who would get into it and not buy the whole trip. In theory, the guru said that we could do whatever we want. On the other hand, there was a definite feeling that you weren't really a devotee unless you actually gave up everything for the guru, including sex."

The totalistic DLM life style is probably the major factor in building loyalty and commitment to the group. "We had the monopoly on truth and love, so that what we were picking up in the outside world wasn't truth. We were told that truth is not in words. Truth is vibration. So we have the truth, and it doesn't matter what we say. Words are not important. You can lie, you can say random words in sequence — it doesn't matter."

There was also commitment through pushing the product. "Whenever we had spare time, we were supposed to be out selling magazines. Most of the people were working in the outside world although they much preferred to work within the organization. We were encouraged to have jobs on the outside: they had to have cash from somewhere. Part of the rationale was that we were functioning in the larger society, we were doing whatever we were doing before, we were proving that we could meditate and be spiritual and still be contributing members of society. But the problem was that there wasn't too much you could do using your mind and meditate very well while you were doing it."

Interestingly, Jim states that the leaders did little meditating. "The people at the top didn't meditate at all. They had to be able to count; somebody had to be able to keep track of the money. Those with strong egos seemed to rise to the top of the organization. They controlled the people by putting them down, jumping on them. And the people would get so hurt that they would start meditating — a lot, turning their minds into jelly beans."

DLM devotees viewed all former associates on the outside as still being "into the darkness." All attachments had to be surrendered, including parents and friends. One of the group's devotional songs, when translated into English, includes this verse: "You are my mother, you are my father, you are my brother, you are my friend, you are riches, you are wisdom, you are my all, my Lord to me." As Jim observes, "You might well say that the guru was your mother and father."

GURU MAHARAJ JI again made headlines in November 1973 when the DLM sponsored a giant festival, Millennium '73, in Houston's Astrodome. Despite extensive publicity, the extravaganza was essentially a flop. Crowds were small, and the financial losses great. In what was billed as the "most significant event in the history of mankind," the guru delivered sat-sang from a blue velveteen throne high above the floor of the Astrodome. An army of premies was brought in from around the country to ensure that all would go well. Jim was among them. "We were all assigned our duties by a computer. I was helping to make twenty thousand tomato and cheese sandwiches. I was operating an electric meat slicer which the organization had rented for slicing tomatoes. After six hours of doing that, I felt the blade going through two of my fingertips. They called an ambulance and rushed me over to the county hospital after asking me, 'Do you have medical insurance?' It required about fifteen stitches per fingertip."

While recovering at home from the accident, which temporarily cost Jim the use of his right hand, his mother contacted Ted Patrick, the deprogramer. "There was no kidnaping. There was no physical force. Mother had Ted Patrick's telephone number by the telephone. I said, 'Mother, you shouldn't have that horrible person's telephone number around. I just read about him in the guru's newspaper.'

"One day, after visiting the doctor's office, I returned home to find a houseful of people, including Ted Patrick. The actual deprograming took only forty-five minutes and consisted of Ted asking me these obnoxious questions and then finally hitting me with the accusation that I'd been brainwashed and hypnotized without my knowledge and consent. I finally bought what he was saying. That was it! He stuck around for three days, but there really wasn't any need for him to do that — he had jolted me right out of it, pretty much, except for the fact that I couldn't stop meditating.

"I had to work on learning to think again. Whenever I would try to think, I'd start meditating. It was like an internal conditioned response. At first I stayed awake all night, because I'd been pretty much conditioned to need to meditate in order to fall asleep."

Several months after leaving DLM, Jim accepted Christ as his Savior as a result of the ministry of the Berkeley Christian Coalition. Today he lives in Southern California and is writing an autobiographical novel. He remains active in efforts to prevent other young people from being caught up in the cults. Jim learned from painful, first-hand experience that all is not sweetness and light in the Divine Light Mission.

◆ Part 2 ◆

Commentary on the Cults

◆ EIGHT ◆

The Seduction Syndrome

TO UNDERSTAND the dynamics of the transformation process by which a young person becomes totally enveloped in an extremist cult, it is important to note the context from which he comes. What kind of background factors characterize the young people who are entering the new-age cults in such alarming numbers? Where are they "at" when they first decide to explore the kinds of groups discussed in Part 1 of this book? Why do they find these groups so appealing? How do the cults manage to control their converts once they have recruited them?

The majority of people who join new-age cults are between eighteen and twenty-two years old at the time of first contact. In other words, the immediate post-high school period is when a potential joiner is most vulnerable, though persons as young as fourteen have become victims. A profile of the typical cult member reveals that he or she is white, middle or upper-middle class, with at least some college education and a nominally religious upbringing. In short, the typical cult prospect fits the image of the all-American suburban boy or girl next door.

To be sure, some young people in the cults come from the margins of society or have experienced very unstable or nonexistent family relationships. But they do not constitute the norm. Most have grown up in average American homes, and many have experienced varying degrees of communication problems with their parents. A number have known the pain and deprivation of a single-parent home, and perhaps for this reason some have strongly identified with older cult leaders

who provide a parental image. Speaking of Victor Paul Wierwille of The Way, one ex-member describes her feelings: "He
was very much the father figure, a strong man, and I just really
fell in love with him. I sort of had a crush on him."

Shelley Liebert, the young woman who became an instructor in the Unification Church, feels that two types of people
pass through the Moonie indoctrination camps. There is the
successful, idealistic, very secure kind of person, who represents the most promising prospect as far as the leadership is
concerned. On the other hand, there are clearly those recruits
who have problem backgrounds and have experienced varying
degrees of "failure" according to the standards of middle-class
America. These young people have dropped out of school, have
been involved in the drug scene, come from broken homes, or
have a history of emotional problems and unresolved personal
conflicts.

Some seekers who had troubled backgrounds did not sur-
vive in the Moonie movement, as Shelley points out. "I always
favored the little stray ones. But they weren't usually the ones
that made it. I knew I was fighting for a lost cause, like when
you bring in a bird with a broken wing — you know it's going to
die, but you take care of it anyway. They were drifters, and they
didn't have the stamina."

Perhaps more than anything else, the young people pursuing cults today are involved in a search for identity and a quest
for spiritual reality that provides clear-cut answers to their
questions. Coming to grips with one's identity has always been
a part of adolescence in America, but today's youth face difficulties compounded by the massive cultural and social up-
heavals that characterize the contemporary world, especially
during the last decade. Much has been written and said about
generational gaps, the alienation of youth from the larger society, the disillusionment and disenchantment with the Estab-
lishment which led to immersion in drugs by some and involvement in radical politics by others. Eastern mysticism,
existential do-your-own-thing philosophies, and a rejection of
many traditional virtues and values have resulted in a confusing array of alternative life styles and value systems which were
not options for young people only fifteen years ago.

Despite the boom in entertainment and the pervasive impact of the mass media, youth often remain bored, unfulfilled, and lonely. This is reflected in the unprecedented geographic mobility of a growing segment of the youth subculture. An army of hitchhikers and street people signify that American youth are running away from something. The old anchorages are increasingly absent, for whatever reasons. The separation from the familiar; the tendency to drift in and out of jobs, college, and sexual relationships; uncertainty and anxiety regarding the future; discontent with economic and political structures — all contribute to isolation and loneliness.

NEVERTHELESS, YOUNG people who have not fled suburbia and their families are also experiencing a crisis of identity. The characteristic ambiguity of adolescence has been compounded in recent years by the liberation ethos that has pervaded our culture and profoundly affected our sex-role relationships. Women's lib, gay liberation, and sexual permissiveness in general stand in contradistinction to the more traditional patterns of the recent past. Appropriate models for adulthood are often unclear or undergoing considerable change. "Even such seemingly universal adult roles as mother and father are amorphous and changing. . . . For youth, therefore, the development of a coherent adult identity and the resolution of generational discontinuities is becoming more difficult," reports Francine Daner in *The American Children of Krsna* (p. 11).

This identity confusion is commonplace among the children of affluence — the chief target of the cults. As an ex-member of the Children of God describes it, "This is such a searching generation, because everything's been so easy for us. Everything's been handed to us. We've never been hungry. It's almost like we're drowned in a sea of possibilities." Or, as Theodore Roszak observes, "Never before has such freedom of choice been available in regard to work, styles of life, and beliefs. Youth may well be victims of the dilemma of over-choice" (quoted by Daner, p. 11).

IF YOUNG people who are potential candidates for the cults are concerned with developing a sense of identity, they are just as earnestly engaged in a spiritual search. Some who were interviewed as part of this study had been pursuing spiritual rainbows for many months and had moved from church to church or even cult to cult in search of firm answers.

A case in point is one young man who, before joining the Hare Krishna cult, had been deeply involved in astrology and occult practices. "At this time in my life I wanted to devote myself to the pursuit of truth. I was seeking God with all my heart. Quite by accident, I met a young man who was a devout member of the Hare Krishna sect. This man's manner of living was the most detached and unearthly that I had ever encountered. He cared for nothing, obviously, but his relationship to God. His detachment and devotion was what really got ahold of me. Here I was, honestly and earnestly seeking God, and this man had found the way."

In *Today's Health* magazine, Max Gunther describes one young woman's spiritual quest — not unlike thousands of her peers. She had been raised a Catholic, but had dropped her religious faith in her early teens. This lack of commitment troubled her as she entered a university in an "uncertain, groping state of mind."

> I thought I wanted to become a nurse but wasn't sure. I thought Christianity meant a lot to me but I wasn't sure of that either. I guess I was kind of desperately looking for somebody who had firm yes-and-no answers, somebody who was sure about things and could make me sure (*Today's Health*, February 1976, p. 16).

During her sophomore year, this same girl encountered a nomadic cult that was combing her campus for converts. She was attracted by the apparent strength of their religious faith and the sureness and calmness of their approach. "I kept going back and asking them questions, and they always knew the answers — I mean really knew them." She joined them and discovered "a world where you had direct, clear, simple rules to tell you how to find salvation. There were no questions, no confusion — and I guess that's what I'd been looking for" (*Today's Health*, p. 16).

The desire for sure, black-and-white answers to life's questions is illustrated in the case histories of Part 1 and is con-

firmed in the experience of other young people who participated in this research effort. Cultic groups like The Way are
very much aware of this perceived need on the part of today's
youth. Victor Wierwille's Way observes, "There is plenty of
religion about us today, but very little logical, accurate, and
effectual principles that answer people's questions. Questions
you have about life can be answered with 'a mathematical
accuracy and scientific precision,' answers that work today, not
in some distance future."

Cults not only provide firm answers to every question, but
also make promises that appeal to those needing reassurance,
confidence, and affirmation. A prime example of this is seen in
a flyer advertising The Way's "Power for Abundant Living"
course and posted on college campuses across the nation. It
announces in bold headlines: BE A WINNER. The passer-by
who is living "below par" is invited to read these lines:

YOU CAN HAVE POWER FOR ABUNDANT LIVING

Abundant living means you can be SET FREE from all fear,
doubt and bondage; DELIVERED from poverty, sickness
and poor health; OVERFLOWING with life, vitality and
zest; RESCUED from condemnation and self-contempt;
CURED of drug and sex abuse. You can RESTORE your
broken marriage; ENJOY a happy united family, where
there is no generation gap.

If you have power for abundant living you can GAIN self-
respect; enjoy SATISFYING work with more than
ADEQUATE income. You can OVERCOME depression,
discouragement and disappointment and have LOVE, JOY
AND REAL PEACE. There can always be a POSITIVE out-
look on life, day after day, with no let down. There can be a
new PURPOSE in your life. If you have the more abundant
life,

YOU CAN HAVE WHATEVER YOU WANT!

Every problem you ever had can be overcome when you are
fully and accurately instructed.

Although some young people who enter cults have little or no
religious background, many have had nominal religious exposure. A few have had extensive experience in traditional
churches or synagogues. Invariably cult seekers have found
these conventional religious institutions to be lacking in spiri-

tual depth and meaning, incapable of inspiring commitment and providing clear-cut answers, and often hypocritical in everyday life. They view the religious life of their parents as shallow and perfunctory. A former cultist remarks, "Looking at Christianity, I didn't see the devotion there that I did in the Hare Krishna movement."

ANY PERSON experiencing an identity crisis or involved in a serious spiritual quest is theoretically vulnerable to the seductive outreach of the cults, but some are more vulnerable than others. On the basis of evidence drawn from the life histories of former members, it is clear that persons who have recently gone through some kind of painful life experience or who find themselves in a state of unusual anxiety, stress, or uncertainty are far more susceptible to cultic involvement.

For example, students just entering that strange and sometimes scary university world are particularly vulnerable to the appeal of a cult masquerading as a warm, friendly group offering fellowship and small-group intimacy to lonely freshmen. An ex-Moonie who was in her first year at the University of California at Berkeley was ripe for such an appeal: "I was really unhappy for a lot of reasons. My roommate and I didn't get along so well. I had a lot of trouble making friends because people at that school are really academic and all they wanted to do was read books. I was feeling basically alone, and then I began to falter in school. I felt like I blew it and couldn't catch up and didn't know what I was going to do. I was frantic."

Other precipitating life experiences that increase vulnerability include such things as a recent divorce of one's parents or similar serious problem in the home; the extended, critical illness of a family member; a break-up with a girl friend or boyfriend; poor academic performance or failure; and unpleasant experiences with drugs or sex. When someone is feeling exceedingly anxious, uncertain, hurt, lonely, unloved, confused, or guilty, that person is a prime prospect for those who come in the guise of religion offering a way out or "peace of mind."

SOME YOUTH have had a single, traumatic life experience that triggers entrance into a cult, but a significant number might be characterized as having chronic emotional or personality problems of a pathological nature. Dr. John G. Clark, a psychiatrist associated with the Harvard Medical School and Massachusetts General Hospital, has spent several years researching the effects of cult membership on the mental and physical health of young people. He concludes that approximately 58 percent of the cult members he has examined fall into this category. In testimony delivered August 18, 1976, before a select Vermont Senate committee in Montpelier, Dr. Clark declared, "These inductees involve themselves in order to feel better, because they are excessively uncomfortable with the outside world and themselves. Such motivated conversions are 'restitutive,' in that the 'seekers' are trying to restore themselves to some semblance of comfort in a fresh, though false, reality."

The remaining 42 percent of the individuals examined by Dr. Clark were found to be normal, developing young people struggling with the usual growth crises of adolescence when, for reasons we have noted, they fell into the trap laid by cults. For the most part, they were strong students facing the expected pains of separation from their families. Dr. Clark reports: "These people tend to be from intact, idealistic, believing families with some religious background. Often they had not truly made any of the major shifts toward independence, and so, left home at the appropriate time believing they were ready for freedom. When this belief was seriously challenged in this brave new world by their first real setbacks or by any real crisis, they became covertly depressed, thus enhancing their susceptibility to the processes of conversion."

Mental health authorities feel that individuals who constitute what Dr. Clark calls the "restitutive group" — those who already have major emotional problems before joining — run the risk of additional damage through prolonged exposure to extremist cults that practice mind control and prevent or inhibit autonomous behavior. The deterioration that may result is analogous to the fate of chronic schizophrenics institutionalized for many years: they eventually lose the ability to think and function with any degree of effectiveness, especially in the outside world.

Even more disturbing is the fact that young people who have no history of mental pathology, and who have relatively normal, healthy personalities upon entering cultic groups, suffer the destructive impact of a very real, very frightening form of thought control or brainwashing that subjugates the will and stifles independent thinking. There is increasing clinical evidence from the various behavioral sciences for the existence of a syndrome of seduction and mental subversion involving cult converts. This is a matter of both great human concern and professional interest.

In many respects, this phenomenon represents relatively unfamiliar scientific ground, as reported by Dr. Marvin F. Galper, a San Diego clinical psychologist. In a paper presented in June 1976 to a group of mental health professionals in Florida, Dr. Galper reported, "We are confronted with a new clinical syndrome. . . . As time passes, anecdotal evidence accumulates in which the established assessment methods of the psychiatrist and clinical psychologist have failed to identify the brainwashed cult indoctrinee."

Although journalists and other observers have questioned the validity of brainwashing claims, a small but growing segment of the scientific community has had sufficient firsthand contact with the phenomenon to conclude that mind control does take place in new-age cults and that the results are tragically evident. As to the potential effects of membership in these cults, Harvard's Dr. Clark warns: "The health hazards are extreme!" On the basis of his own clinical data, he told the select Vermont Senate committee "that coercive persuasion and thought reform techniques are effectively practiced on naive, uninformed subjects with disastrous health consequences. . . . I must also as a physician draw attention to equally, often life threatening, dangers to physical health."

FROM THE Christian perspective, there clearly are spiritual dimensions to the seduction syndrome, and these will be discussed in a later chapter. First we must consider the psychological and sociological components of mind control, or — as some prefer to call it — "coercive persuasion."

The word *brainwashing* is somewhat imprecise, as it has

been variously defined and applied. Nevertheless, it regularly appears in scholarly literature along with more academic-sounding equivalent terms like "thought control," "mind control," "psychological kidnaping," and "coercive persuasion." Brainwashing became a part of the popular vocabulary during the Korean conflict, when American prisoners of war were subjected to psychologically and physically coercive methods of mind manipulation. A number of psychiatric research studies were later published, based on the experiences of POWs. One of the best-known books on brainwashing, *Thought Reform and the Psychology of Totalism*, written by Dr. Robert J. Lifton, is an analysis of techniques used against Chinese intellectuals and Western prisoners in mainland China.

Social scientists have emphasized the very important role that group influences play in thought reform. They have pointed out some striking similarities between what is occurring in the contemporary cults and the brainwashing that took place in China and Korea during the early 1950s. Some also see parallels in the Nazi movement of World War II. Appearing before a group of parents, senators, and other government officials in Washington, D.C., Rabbi Maurice Davis, an outspoken critic of Moon, stated this concerning the Unification Church:

> The last time I ever witnessed a movement that had these qualifications: (1) a totally monolithic movement with a single point of view and a single authoritarian head; (2) replete with fanatical followers who are prepared and programmed to do anything their master says; (3) supplied by absolutely unlimited funds; (4) with a hatred of everyone on the outside; (5) with suspicion of parents, against their parents — the last movement that had those qualifications was the Nazi youth movement, and I tell you, I'm scared.

Lifton and others have noted that "religious totalism" is really just one form of a more general ideological totalism characteristic of the techniques of brainwashing developed by the Chinese Communists. And as Dr. Lifton observes, "Despite the vicissitudes of brainwashing, the process which gave rise to the name is very much a reality.... thought reform has in fact emerged as one of the most powerful efforts at human manipulation ever undertaken" (pp. 4–5).

The comparison between classical Chinese communist thought reform and cultic brainwashing may not hold up in every respect (some have argued, for example, that direct physical coercion is not employed by cultists), but the evidence now at hand indicates that the parallel demands serious consideration. It is our contention that psychologically persuasive techniques and the dynamics of spiritual seduction combine with group forces and processes to cause youth caught up in the cults to accept ideas, attitudes, and behaviors quite foreign to them prior to their involvement in the groups.

We are speaking of a highly emotional, extremely complex phenomenon. Note that in our delineating the process of radical conversion and thought reform, there will always be exceptions in detail or degree. There is some variation with regard to particular cult groups, and of course there will always be some diversity in the response patterns of individuals. Nevertheless, it is our opinion, based on the existing data, that there is a remarkable pattern to the experiences related by ex-members, regardless of the cult. There is ample confirmation from other sources as well — parents, siblings not involved in the cults, journalists, ministers, other professionals — of the kinds of behavior, thinking, and attitudes which will be discussed.

THE TRANSFORMATION of personality and thinking that occurs in the cults includes, as already suggested, a highly seductive process involving individuals who are already quite susceptible. The first crucial element in the syndrome is gaining access to potential converts — recruitment tactics. The cults prey on the kinds of people we have discussed — the lonely, the confused, the idealistic, the searchers. Cultists have an uncanny ability to single out such individuals in a crowd; they seem to sense those who are ripe for the plucking. Frequently, deceitful means are used to entice a young person to make initial inquiry. For example, Moonies will promise a free dinner and lecture without ever identifying the sponsor as the Unification Church. Moon's witnesses have been known to deny flatly any association with the Korean evangelist in their preliminary contacts with potential recruits.

The Children of God, when witnessing on a University of

California campus, were known to circulate in the waiting room of the counseling center, ready to prey on those already identified as experiencing problems. A former member of the Moon movement claims he was instructed to be on the lookout for people wearing backpacks, people on the move. He was also told to avoid Mormons and evangelical Christians — anyone holding firm religious beliefs and possessing substantial knowledge of the Bible was not considered worth the effort. Persons with some religious background and slight acquaintance with Scripture were more promising targets. Moreover, college freshmen and seniors are both viewed as good candidates: freshmen because they are making the transition to an unfamiliar and often unsettling life away from home, seniors because of their insecurity and uncertainty as to future plans.

Once tentative interest has been expressed by the potential convert, intense group pressure and group activity are initiated. Lectures, sermons, Bible studies, and indoctrination sessions — sometimes tape-recorded — are part of a constant round of activity designed to surround the new recruit with an all-encompassing rhetoric. Isolated from prior familiar associations and separated from any input or feedback from the "outside" — while at the same time placed in a position where questioning is discouraged and dissent is not tolerated — the individual is deprived of any opportunity to exercise self-expression and independent thought. He is surrounded by a group of singing, chanting, or meditating peers whose verbal interaction is sprinkled with what Lifton calls "thought-terminating clichés."

Of this constant barrage of indoctrination Dr. Clark observes:

> So intense is this that individuals who are under such pressure and are susceptible tend to enter a state of narrowed attention, especially as they are more and more deprived of their ordinary frames of reference and of sleep. . . . From that time there is a relative or complete loss of control of one's own mind and actions which is then placed into the hands of the group or of individuals who have the direct contact with the individual inductee.

In her study of the Hare Krishna movement, Professor Daner describes a former member who came to the conclusion that devotees were rejecting the mind's ability to think.

> While she was in the movement and was attending *Gita* classes, she would look around at the devotees sitting in the temple chanting japa silently and listening to the lecture, and all she could think of was Orwell's novel *1984*. When she was in the Philadelphia temple where Prabhupada's lectures are played over the loud-speaker system for twenty-four hours a day, she was unable to sleep (*The American Children of Krsna*, p. 76).

All ex-members of extremist cults report having experienced some kind of sensory deprivation — usually food and sleep. Starchy, low-protein diets combined with only four or five hours of sleep each night wear down one's physical and psychological defenses and make a person even more vulnerable to indoctrination. According to Dr. Galper, "Suppression of the individual's rational judgment processes is fostered by sleep deprivation and sensory bombardment. Mobilization of guilt and anxiety in the indoctrinee intensifies this inhibition of judgmental processes and at the same time leads to heightened suggestibility" ("The Cult Indoctrinee: A New Clinical Syndrome," unpublished paper).

The imposition of guilt and fear is basic to the brainwashing process. That a person's eternal destiny will be jeopardized if he abandons the group is a common belief: "If you leave us, you will endanger the salvation of your soul." An ex-Moonie notes, "I was made to feel guilty if I ever wanted to be alone to think."

The co-authors of an article entitled, "Thought Reform and the Jesus Movement," discuss the various dimensions of religious totalism, including the demand for purity or the necessity to place all experience in categories of black and white ("He who is not for me is against me"). They note "that a major emphasis of the demand for purity is to bring out feelings of guilt on the part of the participants. The rigorous standards can seldom be met; the individual nearly always falls short and is left remorseful and repentant (and thus more easily manipulable)" (*Youth and Society*, December 1972, p. 197). The reader will recall Shelley Liebert's statement regarding the Moon movement: "You were always given more than you could do, and you always felt that you never accomplished enough."

Alamo Christian Foundation is a prime example of a cult that effects mind control through fear. The Foundation fosters an intense fear of a wrathful God: "A lot of 'God is Love' heresy is around, and people are blinded to the Truth." The group also preaches an apocalyptic fear that borders on paranoia. A young member of the group once wrote to her parents to warn them about the ZIP codes developed by the U.S. Postal Service — they held sinister implications for a possible future takeover by "commies." She wrote, "They are conditioning us to numbers. They have 'camps' for Christians set up already. When these things begin to happen, they will *happen fast*."

MEMBERS OF extremist cults undergo a dramatic change in world view. Efforts have been made to alter their former attitude toward and conception of the world, the nature of reality, and the ends and purposes of human life. In *The Joyful Community*, a study of the Bruderhof commune, Benjamin Zablocki underscores how difficult it is to effect a change in a person's world view.

> Change in world-view is possible, although rare and difficult. It can occur in a religious conversion and in psychoanalysis. Both of these processes are undergone voluntarily. Classic thought reform, on the other hand, is an involuntary method of changing a person's world-view (p. 247).

In terms of Lifton's analysis of thought reform, this shift in world view is accomplished through a process of resocialization that includes a "stripping process" by which the identity of the individual is greatly weakened, sometimes destroyed. The person is stripped of his personal possessions. In some groups even clothing is communally owned. Frequently the individual's style of dress and appearance is altered to conform to the requirements of the group. The member's sense of self undergoes change as symbols of his former identity are discarded. This is dramatically illustrated in the Hare Krishna movement, where new initiates totally supplant both their personal and social identities.

In order to bring these changes about, a devotee voluntarily subjects himself to a series of abasements, degradations, and profanations of his self. The alienation from his society, from his family and friends begins before an individual becomes a devotee, but entrance into the temple is a formal recognition of this alienation and tends to reinforce it. The devotee's former life is relegated to the status of a dream. . . (Daner, pp. 73–74).

The cultist is stripped of his past. Renunciation and rejection of his prior associations and relationships is mandatory. All connections with family, friends, and the home community are severed. The past must be submerged; reality becomes the present. With regard to Hare Krishna cult, Professor Daner writes, "So deep are the changes that most devotees do not wish to discuss their former lives at all, and the average devotee has to be pressed to reveal any facts of his former life" (p. 74).

A former member of the Children of God relates an incident illustrating the degree to which even mention of the past is reproved: "One time I was traveling with a brother in California and I noticed that there was snow on the mountains. I remarked about their being so beautiful — 'It reminds me of when I skied.' I was rebuked for that, for even mentioning anything at all about what I did when I was not in the Children of God."

Parents are naturally among the first to notice the drastic changes in behavior and attitude after their children join a cult. Their testimony to the characteristic change in identity and rejection of the past is tinged with a sad and anguished realization that they, too, have been relegated to a former category of existence. One parent relates,

The radical change in our son's behavior and personality since he joined this group is hard to believe; he is a totally different person — dehumanized and zombie-like. He has abandoned his entire past life; has no interest in former friends, or in any of his family. His calls and letters are very few and far between, despite our numerous attempts to communicate with him. When we do speak with him, it can never be on a personal level; it's strictly a sermonizing type of conversation. There have been serious illnesses within our immediate family, but his responses have been negative, completely devoid of emotion.

Cultists not only claim to have discovered a new "spiritual family," but in many cases acquire a new name. Some observers suggest that using Bible names or "spiritual" names helps to avoid detection by searching parents and law enforcement personnel. More pertinent to our analysis is the fact that acquiring a new name reinforces the act of severing all ties, familial and cultural. Daner notes the significance of the ceremony at which the Hare Krishna member receives his spiritual name.

> At this time he makes a lifetime commitment, and receives a new spiritual name and insignia. The devotees are aware of and discuss the effects of this ceremony upon the person who undergoes it. "A person really changes when he is initiated and gets his new name. I almost didn't recognize my own husband, he had changed so much," said a young woman. The process of stripping, leveling, and purifying the person to be initiated so that he can take his place in a community of ISKCON is believed to alter his identity in readiness to take on his new identity as a servant of the Lord (p. 77).

Without exception, the parents who contributed to this research effort commented on the drastic, sometimes sudden personality changes they observed in their children. Statements like "He is not the same person" and "She's not the same daughter I once knew" are common. One parent notes, "She changed from a person extremely meticulous in her appearance, thoughtful and considerate of family and friends, to a person completely opposite. Soliciting and peddling up to eighteen hours a day left her no time for personal grooming, proper rest, or nutrition."

Many parents and friends of cult members have also observed changes in voice, posture, mannerisms, and even handwriting. Not only can parents notice a shift in personality and world view in the unfolding progression of letters received from a cultic son or daughter, but some report that the handwriting changes, usually becoming smaller and childish. Misspellings increase and the vocabulary becomes stylized, reflecting the rhetoric of the group and the transformation of the person's thinking. In his testimony before the Vermont Senate committee, Dr. Clark described the abrupt linguistic changes that sometimes occur.

This richness of language is that which parents suddenly miss when they first see their thought-reformed children. Their reaction is appropriately panic! They recognize and correctly identify terrifying, sudden, unacceptable changes in the style of language and the style of relating as well as a narrowing and thinning down of the thought processes. Formerly bright, fluent and creative individuals are rendered incapable in the use of irony or a metaphor and they speak with a smaller, carefully constricted vocabulary with clichés and stereotyped ideas. They also appear to have great difficulty using abstractions in their speech or arguments. They do not love except in clichés and established forms. Almost all of the charged, emotion-laden language symbols are shifted to new meanings.

There is ample evidence that brainwashing as practiced by the cults impairs logical reasoning processes and alters interpersonal relationship patterns. In some extreme cases, individuals have experienced a loss of such basic skills as reading and simple arithmetic. This is most evident in the groups that officially disparage the mind.

FINALLY, THE assault on the convert's prior identity and his subsequently assuming a totally new identity sometimes involve a pattern of personality regression. This is especially the case in the Moon movement, where parents and other observers frequently report that converts have regressed to the level of early teen dependence. A childlike ego state is fostered in the person, and the wholesome innocence of early adolescence appears to be upheld as an ideal. Yet it is unclear whether this childlike status is deliberately encouraged and engineered by the leadership to ensure continued dependence on the group. The scriptural injunction to become like a small child in order to enter the kingdom of heaven is sometimes cited, although cultic use of Scripture can be used to justify a multitude of sins.

Although participation in the cults discussed here nearly always involves substantial personality transformation, it would be an inaccurate generalization to state that *all* cult members display zombie-like behavior or are "spaced-out" robots. Such exotic descriptions *do* seem to apply to some persons, yet journalists and others have tended to overuse the terms. The public relations girls of the Moonie movement, for example, would hardly be able to function in their particular roles in Washington or elsewhere if they walked around in a perpetual trance.

The word *brainwashing* itself may seem harsh and sensational. But to those who have witnessed and experienced the phenomena discussed in this book, the concepts of thought reform and mind control are not abstract, academic speculations. Respected members of the scientific and medical community such as Dr. Robert J. Lifton of Yale, Dr. John G. Clark of Harvard, and Dr. Julius Segal of the National Institute of Mental Health have attested to the clinical reality of the destructive syndrome we have described. All agree that additional research is needed.

Based on his study of young people at various stages of involvement in six different cults, Dr. Clark comes to this conclusion: "The fact of a personality shift in my opinion is established. The fact that this is a phenomenon basically unfamiliar to the mental health profession I am certain of. The fact that our ordinary methods of treatment don't work is also clear, as are the frightening hazards to the process of personal growth and mental health."

◆ NINE ◆

The Characteristics of Cultic Commitment

CULTS ARE sometimes referred to as "high-demand" religious groups, because of the rigorous regimen and the unusual degree of commitment required of members. Every one of the groups we have studied makes extraordinarily high demands of activity on their followers. As Eric Hoffer points out in *The True Believer*, all such groups "demand blind faith and single-hearted allegiance."

Pseudo-Christian cults like the Alamo Foundation and the Children of God proclaim that "Jesus demands *all* — anything less is not enough." Evangelist Billy Graham frequently uses similar phraseology in his preaching, but he means something entirely different. A former member of the Alamo Christian Foundation used biblical language in a letter to her parents to describe the kind of total commitment she was experiencing: "I praise God that the 'zeal of our Father's House has eaten us up.'" She quotes her pastors, Tony and Susan, as saying: "It's a hard life. You lay down your all for Jesus. It's twenty-four hours a day — nonstop."

As we have seen, membership in extremist cults literally entails nonstop activities such as fund-raising, witnessing, chanting, indoctrination, and forced labor. The above-mentioned young woman describes what "giving your all for Jesus" (and the Alamo Foundation) involves in this excerpt from a letter she sent to her parents:

> I work in the kitchen from 11 A.M. to anywhere between 2 and 4 in the morning. We then go home to sleep and get up

at 8 A.M. The days are long and tiring. On our day off we go witnessing from 12 P.M. to 12 A.M. On the witnessing days we get in more rest. The Lord knows how much we can do and gives us strength! Praise God. I've found that tired flesh can be "spiritually" refreshed by fervent prayer. God's Spirit comes down powerfully when the flesh is crucified by fasting and prayer.

In another letter to her parents, this woman describes the progress she is making toward total commitment: "I praise God for the way He stripped me down financially, mentally, etc. in preparation for my serving Him. Right now I'm down to God and me — plus clothes and personals. I believe you're either all for God — or not."

One indicator of cultic commitment is a willingness to strive for goals that seem impossible to achieve. The idea is to exceed the group's expectations, to give more than 100 percent effort. A "shepherd" of a Children of God colony once told his fund-raisers: "God wants you to go out in the field and do more than you're supposed to do. Come back and say that you're unprofitable servants and ask what more you can do." Similarly, in a speech appropriately entitled "Let Us Go Over the Boundary Line," Sun Myung Moon admonished the true believer to "invest yourself until you are consumed." He spoke of the need to push toward the goal, to transcend the boundary.

> You must become more and more successful. If you have been witnessing to people for three hours, you must do more than three hours tomorrow. If you have been doing six hours, more than six hours. And if you have witnessed to 100 people today, you must witness to more people tomorrow. Those are the boundaries you must cross over.

The costs of commitment to the cause of the Unification Church may be considerable, as Moon himself warns. "If we are ready to lose our lives, and if we are doing things at the cost of our lives, we are sure to obtain the goal." At an International Training Session for leaders of the cult in 1973, Reverend Moon discussed the deprivation and sacrifice they should anticipate.

> Never at all dream of living easy and satisfied on the teams. For at least several years you must be ready to clad yourself in rags and feed yourself with humble food and drive yourself out to the battlefield, to fight hard. You will have

no time to make up your face, no rouge, no manicure, and you will be told that you got thinner, your skin has lost its sheen. Will that be all right? Is it your custom to take a bath every day . . . on the mobile teams you may not be able to have frequent baths. . . . You must sleep on the hard cement floor, sometimes. That's too luxurious maybe for you — you must sleep in the jostling van. You are from well-to-do families . . . but in this group you have to go through this bitterness.

While the present life may be a vale of tears and hardships for the Moonies, their leader promises a glorious future in the spirit world. "Even though your life may be a brief one, if you have worked a lot and have been recognized by God, upon entering the other world, you will be welcomed and you will enjoy the flourishing and glorious life there. So, in this life, the question is how hard you work and how much wholesome fruit you produce. So, you must work at the risk of your life and at the cost of your life."

CULTS ARE defined as religious organizations that tend to be outside the mainstream of the dominant religious forms of any given society. In this sense cults are not new to the American religious scene. Nineteenth-century America provided fertile soil for the growth of such culture-rejecting religious communities as the Shakers, Oneida, Amana, Zoar, and the Harmony Society. In a carefully researched and insightful book entitled *Commitment and Community*, sociologist Rosabeth Moss Kanter presents a comparison of the contemporary commune movement and the more successful nineteenth-century utopian communities in America. Dr. Kanter's extensive and systematic research lends itself to an analysis of the extremist cults we have been considering. The similarities between some of the communitarian groups of the 1800s and today's religious cults give credence to the notion that there is indeed nothing new under the sun.

The practice of describing utopian communal units as "families" was common, as Dr. Kanter explains.

Many communities, including Oneida, thought of themselves as one large family, with the leaders often being addressed in parental terms ("Father Noyes") and the members conceptualized as children. For the Shakers, their elders were "gospel parents" and the members "children of the new creation." Members are often "brothers" and "sisters" to one another (p. 46).

In the contemporary commune movement and in some of the new-age cults, the metaphor of the family remains. Dr. Kanter mentions a hippie commune that calls itself the "Lynch family"; there is the notorious "Manson family"; and from the world of the religious cults, there is the "Love Family" and the "Unified Family," the latter being one of the "front" names of the Unification Church. Speaking of the annual August gathering or homecoming of his followers, Victor Wierwille of The Way calls it the "most blessed and joyful family reunion anywhere in the world today."

As we have already seen, there is constant reference in cultic circles to "spiritual parents," "pastors in the Lord," "older brothers and sisters," "babes," and "spiritual children." Jane Berg, wife of Children of God founder "Mo" Berg, is referred to as "Mother Eve." Reverend Moon and his wife are known as the "True Parents," and Moon is addressed as "Father."

Dr. Kanter found that for communes — past and present — the problem of securing total and complete commitment is crucial. The extremist cults we have studied are also, in varying degrees, communal in nature. They too must maintain unswerving loyalty and commitment in order to achieve their goals. They must be able to solve the three problems which, according to Kanter, all such groups face: continuance, cohesion, and control. For the cult to continue to exist, members must be retained and must be willing to carry out the tasks of witnessing, fund-raising, instruction, and daily operation. Someone must be willing to transmit the specialized spiritual knowledge, but someone must also be willing to peel potatoes and take out the garbage. Group cohesiveness refers to the ability of members to "stick together," to develop a common response to perceived threats from the "outside" or from "Satan." And control involves the development of obedience to leaders and unquestioning conformity to the beliefs and values of the group.

There are a number of ways in which current cult groups generate commitment. One reason that so many of today's extremist cults appear to have "staying power" is because they exemplify many, if not most, of the commitment-building processes ("commitment mechanisms") that were found by Dr. Kanter to characterize the more "successful" nineteenth-century communal groups. After extensive research, Kanter concluded that the number and kind of commitment-building processes generated in a given group will determine that group's success — its ability to endure (p. 74).

Kanter's analytical scheme provides a useful framework for understanding the characteristics of commitment seen in the new-age extremist cults. She examines six separate commitment-building processes: (1) sacrifice, (2) investment, (3) renunciation, (4) communion, (5) mortification, and (6) transcendence. We shall discuss each of these commitment mechanisms briefly to demonstrate their application to the contemporary cult groups.

WHEN A YOUNG person is required to make certain "sacrifices" as a test of his faith or loyalty, his motivation to remain in the group rises considerably. All cult programs demand that new recruits "give up" something for joining. They may have to sacrifice a college education, a promising career, or even a potential husband or wife for the "cause." Referring to his own movement as a "family," Sun Myung Moon tells his followers, "You cannot ask your family to sacrifice itself for you; you must be ready to sacrifice yourself for the family." Membership in the Moon cult may preclude the possibility of marriage. The "Master" warns, "You must not think of getting married, because there are a great many things to do."

Celibacy is a requirement or an encouraged ideal in a number of the new-age cults. Interestingly, Dr. Kanter's research found that most long-lived nineteenth-century communities were celibate for at least part of their history. "Communities often ban sexual relations at times in their history when it is especially important that energy and attention be devoted to group tasks" (p. 78).

Membership in a group like the Hare Krishnas means sacrificing attractive clothing, make-up, and other forms of personal adornment. This prohibition can be explained by the cult's ideological disdain for the human body, but it also arises from their practice of separating the sexes and requiring sexual abstinence. According to an ex-member, "The women were dressed carefully so as to cover the ears, the ankles — everything and anything that might give or stimulate sexual desire. The diet was also consciously controlled to eliminate sexual stimulation. This was their reason for providing such a low-protein diet."

An austere life style, without the comforts and affluence of middle-class America, is an effective sacrifice mechanism. Hard work, substandard living conditions, nonindulgence, and little or no monetary reward — all may characterize the committed cultist. New members of the Unification Church are encouraged to fast for seven days. Moon states, "You have to have confidence that you can go and work without eating for seven days." Members of Moon's mobile teams hardly fare better on the road. Ex-members report that fast-food hamburger and chicken restaurants are typical sources of nourishment. To obtain maximum efficiency and effort, Moon once gave this instruction: "You can put some dry food in your pockets, and you can eat as you walk."

THROUGH THE process of investment, cult members' commitment grows stronger. Tangible resources like cars, stereos, bank accounts, and stocks are turned over to the group upon joining. It goes without saying that intangibles like time and energy are transferred to the group to promote its objectives.

Like the utopian groups of the past, extremist cults promote commitment by emphasizing the irreversibility of investment. According to the text of a formal report on the activities of the Children of God conducted by the Charity Frauds Bureau of the State of New York, "No ex-member was permitted to retain any of the possessions he 'contributed' nor to take them out when he left. In view of the brainwashing techniques ... there is a real question as to whether members are exercising their free will when they 'donate' their possessions to the Children of God" (p. 12).

STRONG COMMITMENT is also built by means of renunciation, or "the relinquishing of relationships that are potentially disruptive to group cohesion" (Kanter, p. 82). As discussed in the previous chapter, the process of severing all past associations is a part of the pattern of thought reform common to all cults. After the initial phase of brainwashing is completed, there continues to be an emphasis on disengagement from the old and engagement with the new.

Following Kanter, renunciation usually involves relationships in three categories: with the outside world, within the couple, and with the family. Let us note briefly how the cults regulate and control these relationships to their own advantage.

According to Dr. Kanter, "The outside society, a changing, turbulent, seductive place, poses a particular threat to the existence of utopian communities, so that most successful communities of the past developed sets of insulating boundaries — rules and structural arrangements that minimized contact with the outside" (p. 83). The same is true of religious cults today. Unlike the largely rural communal experiments of the nineteenth century, however, today's cultic movements are very much a part of the urban world. Still, the world outside the cult is viewed as a corrupt, evil place to be ventured into only for proselytizing and fund-raising and other necessities. The threat to new converts is particularly real, and therefore "older" members are required to accompany the neophyte. Most groups have strict rules governing the movement of both members and visitors on their property.

As we have mentioned, some groups maintain facilities that are geographically removed from the "beaten path." Moonies speak of the "farm" or "the ranch" or "the camp" where initial training and indoctrination sessions are held. The Children of God, the Alamo Foundation, the Love Family, the Way, and the ISKCON movement all own properties in isolated areas. Some of them are carefully guarded, especially since the wave of deprogramings started a few years ago.

Specialized terminology and linguistic patterns form what Kanter terms a "psychic boundary" distinguishing the group from the larger society. In-group jargon emphasizes the separation of "them" from "us." Terms like "Systemite," "karmi," "Whore of Babylon," "blooper," and "love-bombing" take on special significance to the insider. It has been reported that Moonies sometimes assume a characteristic linguistic style — a pidgin English — reflecting the large numbers of orientals in the movement.

Of the communitarians of nineteenth-century America, Kanter writes, "Successful groups also tended not to read outside newspapers and not to celebrate national, patriotic holidays; they tried to cut themselves off as much as possible" (p. 84). Again, the same can be said for contemporary cults. Newspapers, TV, magazines, books other than certain "approved" religious literature — all are prohibited in most groups. As one ex-member puts it, "I had to reject my worldly knowledge — foolishness — according to their interpretation of the Bible." Another former member advised her parents: "Keep away from books. God will teach you in *His Word*, which will not pass away."

An incident related by an ex-member of the Children of God illustrates the mechanism of renunciation. In this case it involves a best-selling paperback book widely read in the youth subculture. "One day I just happened to ask one of the brothers if he had ever read the book *Zen and the Art of Motorcycle Maintenance*. He asked, 'What?' So I repeated myself, and he could not believe that I had said that. He asked, 'Was it written by Mo?' I said, 'No.' It completely astounded him that I had even thought to say such a thing. I really thought it was a good book. In fact, at the time I almost thought that it helped lead me to the Children of God. For the next half-hour he recited Bible verses to me about people who are not spiritually attuned with God. I was rebuked for mentioning the book."

Distinctive styles of dress also serve as insulating boundaries, as with Hare Krishna devotees whose saffron robes and hair styles gain attention and promote demarcation from the general population. A former ISKCON member described it this way: "We really felt that we belonged to each other when we were out in public. We needed each other for protection and to reinforce that we felt okay and socially secure. As long as we were together and there was another shaved head or another orange sari around, it was a comfort — because we looked so weird."

Another ex-Hare Krishna member recalls similar feelings of being "cut off" from the rest of the world. "My very dress and outward appearance isolated me. I was living among people who thought, lived, and ate the same way I did. I couldn't relate to anyone outside those I lived with, because I felt extremely out of place with anybody else. Anywhere except in the Krishna temple or in the company of Krishna devotees, I was an absolute freak. The only time I felt socially confident was within our own group."

Cult groups also discourage the formation of exclusive relationships based on two-person attraction or friendship, because such attachments pose a potential threat to the group. As Kanter observes, "Exclusive two-person bonds within a larger group, particularly sexual attachments, represent competition for members' emotional energy and loyalty" (p. 86). An ex-member of the Hare Krishna remembers this form of renunciation very well: "We worked at removing the love relationships between one another in every way possible. What we were trying to do, we theorized, was to direct our love and devotion, not toward people on this earth, but to our conception of God. Such 'worldly attachments' as family and friends stood in the way of complete devotion. Friendship was really discouraged. When I would grow close to one or more devotees through time spent together, the leaders would decide that it would be in the pursuit of Krishna Consciousness for us to work on separate projects or to avoid each other for a while so that we could concentrate more fully on God."

If close friendships represent threats to the cohesiveness and functioning of the cults, so does the family. The renunciation pattern that begins with the initial brainwashing process is continually reinforced throughout one's membership period. Parents are referred to as "the devil in disguise," and relatives are considered to be "just flesh relationships." One ex-cultist states that contact with relatives was seen as "polluting" because "they would discuss things that weren't necessarily relevant to Krishna Consciousness."

Renunciation of family ties likewise characterized some

of the communal religious groups in nineteenth-century America. The following Shaker hymn, quoted in Kanter's book *Commitment and Community* (p. 90), could easily be adopted by today's extremist cults, provided the language were updated:

Of all the relations that ever I see
My old fleshly kindred are furthest from me
So bad and so ugly, so hateful they feel
To see them and hate them increases my zeal
    O how ugly they look!
    How ugly they look!
    How nasty they feel!

Elsewhere in the same hymn, the virtues of the new, "spiritual" family are extolled.

My gospel relations are dearer to me
Than all the flesh kindred that ever I see. . . .
    O how pretty they look! . . .

The charter of the Church of Armageddon (the Love Family) reads: "Our family is the answer to all our hopes. . . . By Jesus Christ each one of us is freed from his narrow, lonely past, and we can finally see clearly that we are all one family, that we belong together." The same document goes on to declare that members of this "spiritual" family are no longer bound by "worldly traditions of matrimony," because they are the "children of the resurrection." The scriptural basis for the declaration is Matthew 22:30, quoted, of course, in the King James Version: "For in the resurrection they neither marry, nor are given in marriage, but are as the angels of God in heaven." It logically follows, says the Love Family, that "worldly marriage is null and void; all worldly relationships dissolve upon joining the Church, because the Church is one family. . . ."

Communal cults, past and present, frequently find that children are disruptive to the community and remove them from the group for rearing or schooling. This is illustrated by the comment of an ex-Hare Krishna member: "The young children were treated like a problem. The people were friendly toward them, but they were not openly or affectionately loved. They were separated purposely from their parents so as to break up family attachment in favor of God attachment."

"COMMUNION" IS the general term Dr. Kanter uses to describe a multiplicity of processes that enhance commitment: "connectedness, belonging, participation in a whole, mingling of the self in the group, fellowship" (p. 93). Working, witnessing, and worshiping together create a powerful "we-feeling."

One effective mechanism for building commitment and a sense of community is to emphasize the importance, not only of the group, but of the individual member. Cults achieve a sense of togetherness both by encouraging team effort and by repeatedly reinforcing the notion that "our team is *the best* of all possible teams." Members are made to feel they are part of a cause that will revolutionize the world. The Moon movement is especially skilled at inculcating this feeling of specialness. An excerpt from "Master Speaks" illustrates how Reverend Moon can make college graduates feel that selling flowers on street corners is something very special:

> . . . your old university friend visits you and looks at your shabby appearance and says, "What happened to you? You are a university graduate and had many things before. Why are you so shabby looking . . . ? You should follow me." You must tell him that you would not take the whole world for this. "Wait five years longer and I will show you." You are a university graduate with a B.A. and other degrees — you are on the street with bundles of flowers, and people may deride you, laugh at you; . . . you can say to yourself, "Those old friends of mine cannot sell flowers on the street like this. If they were given this, they could not do this. But I can do this. I am doing more valuable things than they."

The following quotes from Reverend Moon provide additional evidence of his ability to persuade his followers that they have identified with a cause worthy of sacrifice, worthy of total commitment:

> If you are resolved to live for the cause and die for the cause, you are already being resurrected. You are transcending life and death. God is on our side. . . . you are going to be the incarnation of God.
>
> This movement which I head cannot be stopped. We must present to the youth and mankind of the world the clear-cut explanation of the goal and the way to go. As people recognize the value of the goal, the movement becomes more and more invincible.

This is your mission. . . . I want you to realize that you are summoned as a champion of God for a historical, Messianic mission.

. . . Now that Master is here leading you, if you devote yourself to him, cooperate with him, obey him in every way possible and follow him, you can make the whole world centered in God and there will be no Communists.

Especially with new converts, many cults employ principles of the "power of positive thinking" to build loyalty and commitment to the group. Undershepherds in The Way are instructed to "treat your person with the loving arms of a mother. . . . Don't magnify weaknesses . . . BUT INSTEAD, magnify strong points." Likewise, participants in weekend seminars sponsored by the Unification Church soon learn that they are to affirm the positive and avoid the negative. Instructors will go out of their way to compliment responsive inquirers: "What a pretty scarf you're wearing!" As Shelley Liebert put it, "We had to turn on the charm — all the time."

Moon himself set the tone for his followers in 1965 when he told them, "Be a somebody! Set your own individual goal of perfection, your own standard of achievement. Decide what you best can do, and what you need to achieve your goal — physical, educational, or financial needs. Then fulfill them."

Another effective means of developing a "we-feeling" is to stress the exclusivity of a group's belief system, particularly the path to salvation. The followers of Tony and Susan Alamo believe that only those "saved" at the Foundation are truly saved; all others who claim to be Christians are demon possessed. The young people at the Foundation are persuaded that they constitute "Joel's Army" and that they will have to flee into the wilderness when the Antichrist is revealed: "The world is coming to an end. Why not join the army of the living God?"

The Hare Krishnas are told of God's special love for their group and how the karmis (outsiders) are all being misled by illusion (maya). "By putting them down, we were built up," says an ex-member.

The same kind of "they vs. us" mentality is displayed in the Moon movement. "They haven't the knowledge. You have the Father, you have the knowledge."

Communion and commitment are further accomplished through frequent group meetings and participation in group ritual. "Through ritual, members affirm their oneness and pay homage to the ties that bind them" (Kanter, pp. 99–100). In a ritual held early every Sunday morning, members of the Unification Church pay homage to Reverend Moon in the highly significant "pledge service." It is during this service that new recruits see Moon's picture for the first time. "Then they feel that they've been admitted to the inner sanctum. It's like the final step in the initiation process for a new member; you're allowed to see the Master's picture and allowed to bow down to it."

Persecution, imagined or real, tends to unify people. In the cults a sense of belonging is enhanced and commitment strengthened by what is perceived to be persecution. Many of the groups under consideration here have received a "bad press" — unfavorable publicity. Journalists, investigating legislators, parents, and even sociologists are transformed into "instruments of Satan" by defensive cultists. Susan Alamo has lashed out on her TV program against the "agitators," "Commies," and "troublemakers" who are spreading "wild stories" about the Alamo Christian Foundation. ISKCON denounces the "bewildered, envious, and fearful . . . bigoted individuals . . . making widespread propaganda" against the Hare Krishna movement. Reverend Moon speaks of "negative forces that are trying to stop us and put us on the defensive."

MORTIFICATION PROCESSES are another means identified by Dr. Kanter for building commitment. "One intended consequence of mortification processes . . . has been to strip away aspects of an individual's previous identity, to make him dependent on authority for direction, and to place him in a position of uncertainty with respect to his role behavior until he learns and comes to accept the norms of the group" (p. 103).

Francine Daner writes about the "degradation rituals" which reinforce the notion that a Hare Krishna devotee is the lowliest of the low, an impure, fallen soul. "For this reason he deprives himself of all possessions, renounces everything, and even claims to know nothing. . . . The bodily self is relegated to an inferior, unclean status" (*The American Children of Krsna*, p. 76). The rejection of the individual ego and the physical body is evidenced by the fact that mirrors are virtually nonexistent in ISKCON temples. An ex-member explains that if a Hare Krishna devotee has to look in a mirror, he/she will probably say something to the effect, "O this stupid body!" This is part of the devotee's constant practice of subjecting himself "to degradations and assaults on his identity which are designed to detach him from his former self-concept" (Daner, p. 77).

Interestingly, mirrors were also reported absent from Children of God colonies by the ex-members interviewed by the writer. According to the mother of a former member of the Love Family, the same was true of that group's houses: "Occasionally, when someone would come to visit with a car or a van, she said she would go out and look into the mirror of the vehicle just to see what she looked like."

Assaults on the self in the form of mortification of the body through physical activity and labor are also common in pseudo-Christian cults like the Alamo Foundation. A former member exclaimed in a letter to her parents, "Praise the Lord. He has brought my body under subjection. He strengthens me amazingly since we work some days for 24 hours — then Jesus provides 8 hours sleep the next night." This same young woman later wrote that she had been standing up so long that her legs had started to swell and she was forced to lie down for three days.

Another mortification mechanism involves the use of punishment, embarrassment, or some other means of applying sanctions to "deviant" members. A former cult member reports that someone who didn't measure up to expectations was subjected to subtle shunning: "Sometimes a person could be moved to a distant location against his will, or someone would give him undesirable jobs so that he might take the hint and leave." One ex-cultist spoke of group pressures to conform — especially when it was time to awaken in the morning: "If a person didn't get up on time, people asked him about it and would openly scold him for being tardy. Of course there were always the glances, the condemning looks, when one didn't fully participate."

Dr. Kanter notes, "In successful nineteenth century groups, mortification was also aided by a type of stratification system known as 'spiritual' differentiation, which distinguished members on the basis of their achievement in living up to group standards and taking on the community identity" (p. 108). The same kind of spiritual hierarchy and ranking system can be seen in the contemporary cults. New members are frequently segregated from more "spiritually advanced" members, and degrees of holiness or spiritual attainment are indicated by titles, positions, special wisdom or knowledge, and superior living conditions. Because of their position on the spiritual totem pole, cult leaders often succeed in stretching the rules. Referring to certain ISKCON leaders, a former member stated, "They have a lot of money and their own cars. Their wives have the nicest clothes and the nicest jewelry. Some of them live in trailers outside of the temple, which is equivalent to living in a mansion because they have things like beds, stoves, refrigerators, bathrooms — whereas most Hare Krishnas sleep on the floor."

Again, "a part of the process of commitment is to find a common denominator with other people, to substitute a group-based identity for one based on individual differences" (Kanter, p. 110). Cult groups accomplish this by destroying a person's sense of privacy and uniqueness. The individual ego is replaced by a communal ego. "There was no sense of privacy at any time, and no feeling of uniqueness. You were trying to lose your ego. We were consciously working at losing ourselves in that incredibly intricate code called Krishna Consciousness." Dr. Daner's research reiterates how the lack of privacy promotes mortification in the ISKCON movement:

> The invasion of privacy in temple life is complete and all-pervasive. The devotees are instructed in detail bathroom habits. They are not allowed the use of toilet paper, but are required to take a shower after passing stool. There is no personal privacy, and all bathing and bathroom facilities are open, but segregated by sex. All sleeping rooms are shared, eating is communal, almost all activities are group activities (p. 76).

Infringement of the individual's privacy in some groups includes the censoring of both incoming and outgoing mail. An ex-member of the Love Family confides, "We didn't always get the letters sent us. Sometimes they were confiscated before we got them. One time I got a letter from a friend which had been opened before I received it. Love [the cult's leader] wouldn't let me reply to it. He asked one of the men to answer it."

According to an investigative report released by the Office of the Attorney General of the State of New York, Children of God elders were known to intercept mail addressed to members who either never received the letters or received them with portions deleted. The report states that "checks were cashed and the contents of packages confiscated without the addressee's knowledge or permission." COG members had to leave all outgoing mail unsealed, to allow for censorship and posting by designated leaders. COG elders also kept a log of all incoming phone calls and made notes regarding the caller's "attitude." According to the New York report, "Conversations were taped without the knowledge of the other party and often times amplified in order to prompt the member's responses."

LASTLY, KANTER argues that successful communal groups have built strong commitment through transcendence, ". . . which gave meaning and direction to the community by means of ideological systems and authority structures" (p. 126). The experience of transcendence enables the member to find himself anew in something larger and greater. The sense of being connected with a transcendent moral order is conveyed to the individual through an often elaborate ideology or belief system, as well as through the charisma and authority of a powerful leader.

Contemporary cults provide a well-defined structural and ideological context for searching youth. The various belief systems, though devious from the standpoint of orthodox Christianity, provide purpose and meaning for the individuals involved and legitimate the demands made on members by the group. Every aspect of the totalistic life style of cultists, including free time and recreation, is directed by comprehensive ideological guidelines laid down by the group. This parallels the experience of nineteenth-century religious communes: "Every bit of daily life was infused with the group's philosophy.... Shaker programming extended even to such minor activities as dressing: the right shoe, right glove ... were to be put on first.... The daily routine was minutely programmed" (Kanter, p. 121). New converts in some of today's extremist cults report having to ask permission to go to the bathroom.

All religious cults, whether from the historical past or the 1970s, have strong central leaders who determine spiritual and structural guidelines and are the ultimate source of authority. "Many communities were founded by charismatic figures who were supposed to have access to special sources of power, who served as the link between members and those higher sources of wisdom and meaning, who represented for their followers the greatest growth to which a person could aspire, who symbolized in their person community values, and who inspired devotion, awe, and reverence in their followers" (Kanter, pp. 116–17). The personal magnetism of one such nineteenth-century utopian leader, John Humphrey Noyes of Oneida, has been described as follows: "He has mastered the art of so controlling his disciples that they think they are carrying out their own ideas when they are really executing his designs ... His will is supreme" (Kanter, pp. 116–17).

The latter quote can readily be applied to any of the present-day cult leaders we have discussed. Perhaps no one epitomizes the qualities of a charismatic, authoritarian leader more than Sun Myung Moon. He is intoxicated with self-confidence and has set himself up as the supreme role-model for his followers. "This Master of yours has disciples who are ready to sacrifice their lives for this great cause.... Out of all the saints sent by God, I think I am the most successful one ... as it now stands.... You can trust me as your leader ... I am a thinker, I am your brain."

Moon's sense of self-importance and arrogance is such that he once said to his followers: "Look up to Father saying, 'Everything that he does I am going to do. I am even going to look like him, walk like him and smile like him!'" If Moon is able to elicit even some of this behavior in members of the Unification

Church, it is easy to understand why they are frequently referred to as his "puppets."

ONE THEME seems to be present in one form or another through all the commitment mechanisms we have described. That focal theme is regimentation and discipline. Total commitment is nurtured in a control-oriented environment and manifested by an unyielding discipline. Whether it results in mind control or is present in something as innocuous as physical fitness exercises, the element of strict discipline is pervasive. It is the hallmark of cultic commitment: "Be disciplined." "Drive yourself." "Go like mad for Jesus!" "Control your thoughts."

Rigid discipline and the kind of hyperactivity and tension it is capable of producing in the life of the cult convert probably explain one final characteristic of commitment that is physiological in nature. A serendipity in my research is the fact that, without exception, every female interviewed had experienced an interruption or change of some kind in her menstrual cycle. Comments like these are typical: "I didn't have my period for nine months. I talked to other girls in The Way, and they had said in the Bible it was supposedly unclean to have your menstrual periods in these days, and they were believing God that they would not have their periods." "Just a little while after I joined the Children of God, I had a period, and one of the girls thought that was exceptionally strange, since most of the girls, after joining the group, don't get their menstrual period for a long, long time. Most of the girls I knew had not had periods for two years."

We have taken note of the various dimensions of commitment characterizing extremist cults today. Commitment is a commendable trait; it is a good word. But unrestrained, indiscriminate, unevaluative commitment can be very self-defeating. When it is coerced, it can be self-destructive. The requirements of cultic commitment are often irrational, as illustrated by this command of Reverend Moon: "You must always be ready and on your toes all the time — asleep, awake, in the bathroom or anywhere. When you are called, you must dash out and do your work." That is what is meant by total commitment.

◆ TEN ◆

The Plight of the Parents

"UNLESS IT happens to you, you can't possibly imagine the anguish of losing a son or daughter to one of the extremist religious cults!" That sentiment, expressed by a New Jersey physician in *Medical Economics,* is echoed by thousands of parents throughout America who have experienced heartache, confusion, and anger as a result of first-hand contact with destructive cults. The average person, having heard or read media accounts of "strange" religious cults, usually does not really understand either the magnitude or the seriousness of the cult problem until a family member or personal acquaintance becomes involved. Terms like "mind control" and "deprograming" evoke detached curiosity until the cult phenomenon strikes close to home.

What would be your response, as a parent, if one day you should receive a letter like this in the mail?

Dear Mom and Dad,

I don't know if you know that I have left [name of midwestern city]. But the Lord led two Christian brothers to town, and I feel the Lord led me to go with them and serve the Lord, leaving all material possessions I had, except for what I needed. We have gathered with the others in the Lord, and it was good to meet the sisters in the church. We go by no name, but we are Christians living the way the Bible teaches, clinging only to the Lord.

We dress modestly as the Lord teaches — the women in long skirts and smocks and the men in long robes — hand-sewn by the women. The Lord provides us with food.

We travel all over to speak to souls about the Lord. I have found a real peace, nothing like I could find living in the world.

I have read and read in the King James Version of the Scriptures and just have not found a reason to come back and live a life serving man or going to school to get some degree of carnal knowledge. I always thought that God was leading me to work at the dentist's office and leading me to go to beauty school. But His will is that we *live for Him* and tell others of Him. That is my purpose now, and I pray God will give you grace not to worry about me.

It's really a blessing to live separated from the way of the world. I'm sure you have a lot of questions and many people don't understand how we can actually live by faith and take no thought of what we will eat or drink or wear tomorrow. But I haven't gone hungry or been unclothed yet. We've found the world to be very wasteful. Grocery stores that throw out good food — still packaged, sometimes cold milk, yogurt and cottage cheese, much fruit and vegetables and bread, donuts ... it's truly amazing. We have also been out in the wilderness and the Lord has provided — so we don't depend on these stores. We depend on the Creator!

I just don't feel I can or should explain everything to you. I just pray that the Lord will start to open your eyes to the way the world is falling. Christians need to get out of it. Praise God. There is a lot of persecution to endure, but the Lord's always faithful if we're true to Him. When I was living in the world I kept thinking that there's got to be a way to live by faith and do as the Word says. But I never thought it was possible until I stepped out on a limb and left with those two brothers who were passing through town. When I saw them, I thought they looked like disciples, or how I had visioned disciples in the Bible — robes, sandals, beards. I found they were really following the Bible. I have had the Bible pounded into me all my life and never really understood how it could apply to my life until now. Praise God.

I've found that when one is living according to the Scriptures and not the laws of this world or the tradition of men, persecution is here. We've had some thrown in jail for serving the Lord, some put in mental institutions, accused of being insane, and some set down in front of psychiatrists to try and get this brainwashed way of life out of them. We've had many lies told about us and you may have even heard some on TV. It's very sad to this soul, because so many are rejecting God in persecuting us.

I pray that this letter makes sense to you; I write with much hope that you'll understand. I know it must be hard, because you miss this flesh of your daughter, but I hope you begin to realize that this flesh will pass away and this soul will live forever. I'm just doing what I feel is right for this soul.

I pray that I have not preached in this letter, as it doesn't seem to be the woman's place. I only want you to have a good understanding of what I'm doing, as we've seen many parents deceived and really fight God's work in a life.

I know you miss me and my flesh, and with the worldly holidays coming up I'll probably be missed more. But it's all going to make sense to me on judgment day — praise God. Those celebrations, those gifts are going to mean nothing, and though this flesh is lustful and wants riches on this earth, the soul is blessed to leave it behind. I don't know what happened with the stuff I owned back there. It can be sold or thrown out as far as I care — or given away. I didn't want it to be a burden for people, but when I saw the light I just had to leave before Satan confused me and snared me to stay in the comforts of the flesh.

I will call or see you when the Lord leads me to.

As He leads,
I'm in His care

The themes that appear in this letter are all too familiar to the student of extremist cults: rejection of the "ways of the world," the attraction of an exotic life style, perceived persecution, discovery of the "answers" or "seeing the light," deprecation of "worldly" knowledge and vocations, separation from parents and past, and a pervasive subjectivism. An analysis of letters, notes, and diaries of former cult members reveals the same kind of patterns in virtually all the cults.

In a statement prepared for national legislators, the parents of an ex-Moonie describe the shock they experienced upon learning of their son's activities:

We would like to ask the congressmen and senators . . . to imagine what it would be like to have their son or daughter take a trip across the country after graduating college, planning to return home at the end of a stated time, to resume the life and career for which they had been preparing . . . and then to receive a phone call from an unspecified place three thousand miles away, from someone who sounds only vaguely like the son (or daughter) they knew so well only a few months before, but whose voice is the voice of a ventriloquist's dummy, who speaks to them only in the stilted phrases of a religious pamphlet, who seems to have no recollection of the twenty-odd years of mutual caring and struggling and tears and laughter that makes a family . . . and who cannot answer the simplest question without consulting some unknown person standing beside him!

MOST CULTS are opposed to traditional educational institutions. Parents of victims relate similar stories of children dropping out of high school, college, and even graduate or professional school. "Our daughter was in graduate school, just a few hours from her master's degree. One of her professors persuaded her to attend several meetings of this cult, and as a result, she became a dedicated member, dropped out of school, moved into their commune, handed over her bank account, automobile, etc. Total commitment is expected of each convert, with no time for friends or family, even on special occasions. Although in the same city for almost two years, we seldom saw or heard from her."

Some parents manage to visit their children, though they are rarely alone together. Such encounters are usually strained and unnatural. "On the few occasions when we have been together, both in Detroit and on the West Coast, she is constantly on a treadmill, always running, busy with many 'duties' and 'obligations,' and always fighting fatigue. She has vague, memorized answers to all our questions."

Another parent states, "We asked our Moonie son which restaurant he would like to go to for Thanksgiving dinner, to which he replied, 'Why don't you give me graham crackers and donate my share of the bill to Unification?'"

As detailed in the case history of Lisa Bryant, parents are sometimes prevented by cult leaders from having any contact with their children. Or, attempted communication by letter or telephone is thwarted. Ex-members of the Children of God have said that letters to their parents were sometimes delayed before being mailed, and in some cases were never mailed so as to forestall any immediate parental contact. To avoid parental detection, letters were sometimes mailed from locations other than where written, as reported by a former member of the COG: "They told me I should write a letter to my parents and mail it out [in Manhattan] before I got on the bus to go to New Haven. . . . I should write a letter telling my parents I was no longer with the Children of God . . ." (*Final Report on the Activities of the Children of God*, Office of the Attorney General of the State of New York, September 10, 1974, p. 43).

A number of parents have experienced physical violence at the hands of cult members. A Southern California mother filed a personal-injury suit against the Alamo Christian Foundation after receiving a severe beating during a visit to the premises. She later received a phone call from a member of the Foundation declaring that the beating was just a "warning" and should any further action be taken, the rest of the family "would be taken care of." A woman whose son was formerly with the Hare Krishna cult alleges that "they tried to kill my husband at the Atlanta temple. They pulled him from the street into their yard and sat on him and kicked and clawed him like cats. Then they had our son sign a kidnaping warrant against his father."

THE NIGHTMARE for parents doesn't always end once their child is freed from a cult's grip. After rescuing their son from the Moon movement, one family experienced harassing phone calls around-the-clock. They obtained an unlisted number, but the calls continued.

> When Chris didn't answer or return the calls, the Moonies began threatening Betty and me — threats we took seriously enough to hire around-the-clock armed bodyguards. Even with this precaution, the Moonies kept our house under constant surveillance. One night we discovered that someone had deliberately set fire to the back of our house. Then one afternoon, feeling the house was safe, we all went out shopping and returned to find the house had been broken into and the wires from a burglar alarm system we had installed that same morning had been ripped out (*Medical Economics*, November 1, 1976, p. 80).

DURING THE EARLY seventies, when cult groups proliferated across America, increasing numbers of parents became unsettled about the bizarre behavior displayed by their children in these groups. They turned to ministers, counselors, psychologists, and lawyers for advice. For the most part, they received unsatisfactory responses. People found it difficult to believe some of the strange accounts that parents were reporting. Unfortunately, few individuals — including professional and academic people — seemed to understand the plight of the parents.

A mother, observing drastic personality and behavioral changes after her daughter had joined a cult, telephoned the student development office of the West Coast University where the young woman was enrolled. The mother was concerned and perplexed and seeking guidance. The administrator with whom she talked brushed off the daughter's involvement with the group as probably no more than a passing fad. In essence, he concluded, "Your daughter's 'got religion'; you should be glad she's not into drugs." Undoubtedly this university official was not aware of the potentially destructive implications of cult membership.

Parents have also been frustrated in their interaction with law enforcement personnel and public officials. Fearing unwarranted government intrusion into the matter of religion, law enforcement officials have been reluctant to become involved. Even in instances where there appears to be evidence of child abuse, fraudulent misrepresentation, drug use, or other violations of the law, parents complain that police and district attorneys are cautious or uncooperative. "They are a nonprofit religious organization, and we can't touch them" is often the response. The attitude of some parents is summed up in these comments by a mother whose minor daughter was exploited by the Love Family of Seattle: "We are very angered to think that a part of our society can live this way and actually force themselves upon others, particularly a child of fourteen, use her sexually, and continually feed her all these drugs, and that as parents you're not able to do anything about it, really."

Because of their desire to raise consciousness levels regarding destructive cults, and in order to provide assistance to troubled family members, parents across the United States have banded together in recent years to form a network of grass-roots organizations whose membership is growing. The first such group was organized in San Diego in 1971 and called itself "The Parents' Committee to Free Our Sons and Daughters from the Children of God Organization," later shortened to "FREECOG." With requests for assistance coming from throughout the United States and Canada, as well as abroad. FREECOG went national in February 1972.

It soon became apparent that parents with children in the many other cults springing up were also needful of counsel and basic information about the nature of cultic activity. The administrative and financial load on FREECOG became too great. During the last week of September 1974, a group of people from throughout the U.S. and Canada met in Denver to form an organization known as the Citizens Freedom Foundation. The basic purpose of CFF is to inform the public and to assist parents and victims "through charitable medical, legal, educational and other established facilities."

Besides the Citizens Freedom Foundation, there are currently several other organizations that provide information and advice for parents. These include Citizens Engaged in Reuniting Families; Return to Personal Choice; Citizens Engaged in Freeing Minds; Free Minds; and the Individual Freedom Foundation. Some publish newsletters and sponsor public meetings featuring ex-cultists, researchers, and those involved in rehabilitation efforts. Increasingly the parents' groups are coordinating efforts to press for investigation of fraudulent activities and other violations of the law by cults.

The parents' organizations serve an important supportive function for distressed parents who feel guilt and anger. They become aware of the fact that they are not alone in their struggle. A newsletter encourages: "Never give up. Do not grieve like men who have no hope. If each of us carries a share of the burden, we will succeed. Never let yourself forget that."

THE SAD tragedy of a separated family is documented in the pages of the CFF newsletter of February–March, 1976. The photograph of a smiling young woman is captioned, WHERE IS LISA??? The parents state, "We have special reason to believe our daughter Lisa is involved with the Children of God movement and would appreciate your help in locating her. She disappeared on Jan. 26, 1974. Red hair, brown eyes, fair complexion, 18 years old. Please call collect."

In February 1976 more than three hundred parents and ex-members of cults gathered in Washington, D.C., for a "Day of Affirmation and Protest." A meeting between a panel of government officials and concerned members of the public was held in the Senate Caucus Room with the intention of persuading lawmakers and members of the judiciary to investigate the Unification Church and other groups. The session was convened by U.S. Sen. Robert Dole of Kansas, who had been petitioned by 14,000 Kansans to investigate the activities of the Moon organization.

Although Senator Dole made it clear that the session was not a congressional hearing, the invited participants raised questions and presented testimony which the sponsors hope will generate action at both state and federal levels. Speakers suggested that the Moon movement is as much a political unit as it is religious. With subsequent revelations in the national press about the so-called "Korean Lobby" and its possible ties to Moon staff members like Col. Bo Hi Pak, it would appear that the efforts of the concerned parents will not go unrewarded.

Those presenting testimony at the Washington meeting questioned whether a group like Moon's should have tax-exempt status and whether it can qualify for funding from the Department of Health, Education and Welfare. Speakers also asked about the legality of Moon followers' selling candles, candy, and flowers on the streets while allegedly claiming the money raised is used for drug rehabilitation programs or other charitable purposes.

The *ad hoc* national committee that organized the Washington forum presented its basic position in this statement:

We AFFIRM: 1. our love for our youth;
2. our loyalty to our government;
3. our support of our families;
4. our belief in time-proven religious faiths;

      5. our confidence in American education;

      6. our trust that our society can and will respond to human needs.

We PROTEST: the destructive cults and their strategy of alienation — the alienation of psychologically kidnapped youth from their:

      1. government;

      2. families;

      3. prior religions;

      4. education;

      5. society and its viable values.

The intense feeling and emotion that characterize the experiences shared by participants is conveyed in these comments excerpted from one parent's testimony:

> I come before you as one parent, representing the thousands of parents unable to be with us today. At this very moment, there are parents across this country who are angered, frightened, confused, in despair, because a strange and dangerous phenomenon is happening for which most American parents find no previous experience to turn to for guidance.

> How can parents cut through the invisible barrier that isolates their children from free and open contact with their families? How can parents combat an atmosphere that combines isolation, curtailment of letter writing or telephone calls, fear, and a breakdown of trust in parents? This breakdown of trust is accomplished by indoctrination in Unification Centers of a constantly repeated concept of everyone out there being influenced by a Satan and a threat that if they leave the Unification cult, they or someone in their family will die a terrible death. What a horrifying instrument of fear, guilt, and superstition to implant in a person's mind!

> Who can parents turn to when they realize their children have been instantly enslaved by Moon and his well-paid army to sell peanuts, flowers, and candy from ten to nineteen hours a day, lying to fellow Americans by pretending the money goes for non-existent social welfare purposes?

> You call your lawyer or legislative representative and learn that this evil man, Moon, has on the surface, totally kept within the law. The umbrella of religious freedom serves his church and he carefully only admits those over eighteen years of age.

The time is now to investigate the rapid and mysterious growth of Moon. And I and many thousands of parents come to you today to ask your help, advice, concern, and action to help us to find crucial answers, solutions, and protection to fulfill the most basic responsibility of parents: to protect their children from destruction.

Some critics contend that the cults become scapegoats for the problems of parents, and they tend to react in a desperate and hysterical manner. According to Dr. Irving Zaretsky of the University of Chicago:

Young people get involved with such groups because they want to get involved. How it affects their home life depends on the relationship with their parents. The parents feel helpless when all of a sudden there is nothing they can do about it. What little information has been available through the media has simply reflected parents' concerns back to them. They seize upon the mind control because it is handy to condemn something like this that they have little information about and fear a great deal (Human Behavior, October 1976, p. 49).

Whether or not young people get involved in the cults because "they want to get involved" depends on how you evaluate the syndrome of seduction and brainwashing that we have already discussed at length. If you discount the mind-control argument and assert that members of extremist cults are exercising freedom of choice and have not been manipulated, it logically follows that thousands of parents (and ex-cult members) have deluded themselves and are misrepresenting the facts. However, it is my firm conviction that anyone — professional or lay person — who has had sustained and extensive first-hand contact with the phenomena we are discussing will come to the conclusion that mind control (or whatever label is preferred) is real and that the will to be self-determining is absent. Psychologist Kevin Gilmartin admits in Human Behavior magazine that "it's an amazing process. I know when I first got exposed to it, if someone had told me what I'm saying right now, I never would have believed it."

While it is foolish to deny that some parents of cult joiners have personal and family problems, it seems equally unfair to label parents as the prime problem. To conclude that parents' organizations are "showing signs of mass hysteria," as some critics have stated, is to reveal a shallow knowledge of a complex phenomenon that is causing vast numbers of people to feel hurt and despair — for valid reasons.

PERHAPS THE single most discussed and misunderstood topic in the battle against the cults is deprograming. Persuaded that it is an absolutely necessary step, parents have forcibly removed their offspring from the cults in carefully planned "rescues" or "kidnapings." When such forced removals first came to the attention of the public a few years ago, deprogramers like Ted Patrick assisted parents in the actual abducting and then took charge of the process of reversing the cult's "programing." Because of a series of legal skirmishes involving charges of illegal restraint and kidnaping, deprogramers now leave the abducting to the parents and concentrate their energies on the deprograming itself.

The accounts of what actually transpires during deprograming are varied and confusing. Some journalists have described marathon "counter-brainwashing" sessions lasting twenty hours or more, during which the seized individual is driven to hysteria and then breaks down. Horror stories abound, especially in the cults themselves, about the alleged brutal techniques used by deprogramers to force the helpless victim to disavow his cultic beliefs. An article written by former *New York Times* reporter John McCandlish Phillips (whose own group, The New Testament Missionary Fellowship, has been called cultic) and published in the November 1974 issue of *Christian Life* magazine, came down strongly against deprograming. The article, which also depicts the Alamo Foundation in a favorable light, was reprinted and distributed — without the publisher's knowledge or consent — throughout Southern California by members of the Alamo cult.

Even though the language used by certain deprogramers may be offensive and some of their tactics and judgment may be validly questioned, there has come into being a virtual mythology about deprograming that beclouds the major issues. Stories about bright lights being kept on for twenty-four hours a day or young people being deprived of sleep or food while undergoing deprograming are often distortions of the facts. It is true that many young people resist the attempts made by the deprograming team to have them rationally confront the beliefs and practices of the cult leaders. And it is also true that such exchanges between deprogramer and cult victim may be lengthy and intense. But to charge that deprogramers use the same tactics as the cultists reveals a basic misunderstanding of how the cults operate and a lack of knowledge as to the objectives of deprograming.

Probably the best description of what deprograming entails was stated in *Eternity* magazine by William O. West, who went through the process himself:

> Deprogramming aims at breaking the chains of fear, guilt, and repetitive thought, and at forcing objective evaluation of the unexamined beliefs that were injected into the victim's unresisting mind by the cult leaders after the behavioral chains were originally established. The examination of what the person already believes is the deprogrammer's goal, rather than trying to force him to adopt a new belief. Deprogramming neutralizes the mind (September 1976, p. 75).

In short, the primary aim of deprograming is to assist the individual to think for himself, to penetrate the mental fences that the cult has so effectively constructed. If the victim of mind control cannot see the problem, he/she cannot deal with it. "The individuals are held against their will because the cognitive and volitional state known as will is removed from the individual," explains psychologist Kevin Gilmartin (*Human Behavior*, October 1976, p. 47).

CRITICS OF deprograming charge that the practice violates the cherished American principle of religious freedom which provides the right to believe any religious idea and to affiliate with any religious body. The National Council of Churches has officially gone on record as condemning deprograming: "The Governing Board of the NCC believes that religious liberty is one of the most precious rights of humankind, which is grossly violated by forcible abduction and protracted efforts to change a person's religious commitments by duress." An editorial in the November 1976 issue of Church & State concludes that "kidnapping for the purpose of forcing a person to change his or her religious beliefs not only violates a person's right to be free of physical restraints but also violates that person's most basic right, the right to think and believe without coercion" (p. 22).

Ironically, it is precisely this "right to think and believe without coercion" that is championed by the parents who engage the services of deprogramers. That the opponents of deprograming do not accept the contention that young people are being brainwashed is evidenced by the above-mentioned Church & State editorial, which continues: "... No one has proven that any of the groups targeted by the deprogrammers have used kidnapping or classical brainwashing methods to make converts. So the extreme 'remedies' applied by the deprogrammers are worse than the 'disease' they try to cure" (p. 22). As regards deprograming, the editorialist concludes: "Let us bury it before it buries our liberties."

Such comments only underscore what is already obvious: deprograming and mind control are emotion-charged issues. To some it will be difficult ever to present convincing "proof" of brainwashing. On the basis of my own research, I would argue that the question is not whether one enters a cult group freely, but whether one is capable of exercising free will after a period of time elapses and one has experienced the process of spiritual and psychological seduction. An observation by Mark Rasmussen in his article, "How Sun Myung Moon Lures America's Children," is perceptive in this regard: "Somewhere along the line, for many church members, there seems to be a very real loss of will. While at first the blind commitment to Moon seemed a choice they wanted to make, after a number of weeks they find they don't quite know what they are doing or why they are doing it" (McCalls, September 1976, p. 175).

The parents whom I have met and interviewed wholeheartedly support freedom of religion — but they reiterate that the First Amendment also guarantees freedom of thought. Their position is echoed by Tucson attorney Michael Trauscht, who is quoted in *Human Behavior* magazine as stating, "Freedom of thought is involved, not freedom of religion, because the kids when they are victims of mind control don't have freedom of thought and this is a direct violation of their constitutional rights to freedom of speech and freedom of association" (October 1976, p. 48).

There are young people who have had negative experiences in connection with deprograming. However, the sample of young people I interviewed all viewed deprograming as a necessary and basically positive experience. One participant in the study summarized the feelings of many: "As a result of my experience, I feel I am a much stronger person, and I think if one is deprogramed properly, this usually is true. The guilt factor can break a person like so much thin glass. One is told, one way or another, that he will 'go to hell' if he leaves the cult. The degree of mind control the group possesses over the individual does not allow this fact, which occupies a large part of his consciousness, to escape. Until this control is broken, the individual is very miserable and feels lost, like a cloud blown astray. Unless he is deprogramed or similarly counseled, he walks on ice, thin ice."

A valid criticism of much of the deprograming being carried out currently is that the personnel involved have little or no professional background or training. The various teams of deprogramers now active in the United States and Canada consist mainly of ex-cultists themselves and concerned citizens familiar with the cult scene. The former are especially successful because of their age and relating skills and their personal experience with cult phenomena. Psychologists and psychiatrists are understandably reluctant to enter a situation where the person needing help has been abducted and is therefore an unwilling patient. As a result, there have been instances in which persons having serious emotional or mental problems have received inadequate, if not damaging, assistance from well-meaning but professionally unskilled deprogramers. On the other hand, examples can be cited in which youthful ex-members of cults have been more successful in rehabilitating cultists than highly trained professionals.

OPPONENTS OF deprograming have expressed what is, in the writer's opinion, an unrealistic fear that the phenomenon will somehow snowball into a movement directed at any and all unpopular or "undesirable" religious and political groups. Again, the Church & State editorial demonstrates this concern: "Tomorrow the deprogrammers may be employed by Protestant parents to prevent a child from becoming a Catholic, or by Catholic parents to block a child from converting to a particular Protestant faith" (November 1976, p. 22).

Yet it must be remembered that in order to be deprogramed, one must first be "programed." Except for the rabid anti-religionist, it would be most difficult for someone to build a rational case for brainwashing vis-a-vis any conventional religious group. The campus chapter of Inter-Varsity Christian Fellowship or the Newman Club can hardly be compared with the Children of God or the Moon movement. To suggest that traditional religious groups will shortly become the targets of deprogramers is an insult to the vast majority of American parents and reveals a lack of insight with regard to the distinction between true, self-willed religious conversion and coercive conversion.

A major fault of some deprograming teams has been their tendency to perform the services for which they were hired and then withdraw from the scene. The period immediately following a deprograming experience has the potential for personal disaster unless the ex-member is fortunate enough to have a loving, supportive family or friends who see the need for and can provide the right kind of assistance in the crucial period of readjustment. To deprogram an individual and then "drop" that person amid a spiritual and social vacuum is to leave a problem only half-solved.

In any event, the word deprograming is probably no longer a very useful term, because of the controversy that surrounds it. Although deprogramers themselves no longer participate in the actual kidnaping or abduction of cult victims, their activities still bear the stigma of illegality and unprofessionalism. Many of the newer deprogramers, in effect, are engaged in nothing more than informal counseling, yet the term deprograming retains an image of something far more harsh. Perhaps a better word to use would be, simply, "rehabilitation" or "resocialization." For those preferring a medical or clinical model, the concept of "reality-inducing therapy" may be adequate.

Whatever the label employed, efforts are clearly needed — within the bounds of existing law — to assist young people, in a context removed from the controlled environment of the cult, to evaluate fully and freely the demands and dimensions of the cultic experience. How to provide this opportunity for someone unwilling or unable to leave the cult temporarily remains a perplexing problem.

One promising possibility is the use of the legal conservatorship, which enables parents legally to remove a child over the age of eighteen from a cult by means of a court order. In order for parents to obtain custody of the cult member in this manner, a judge must be persuaded that the mental and physical well-being of the individual is sufficiently jeopardized to warrant such action. The conservatorship is usually limited to a stipulated period of time, during which the parents attempt to secure professional help and/or the services of deprogramers.

TO DATE, relatively few parents have elected to go the conservatorship route, either because of the difficulty involved in obtaining a court order or because of the considerable cost of legal services. The financial drain on parents who attempt to extricate their children from cults — whatever the method used — is tremendous. Fees charged by deprograming teams vary, but $1,500 to $2,000 is not unusual. (Transportation and other expenses incurred by the deprogramers are usually included in the fee.) If parents choose to pursue a conservatorship, legal and other related expenses could run several thousand dollars more. When travel and time away from the job are included in the cost to parents, a total figure approaching $10,000 is not unreasonable. I have talked with parents who have had to mortgage their homes in order to cover expenses. What about parents who cannot afford such large sums of money?

Some young people are so emotionally messed up when

they leave the cults that psychiatric hospitalization is necessary. An example of such a case is poignantly described in the July 1976 issue of *Seventeen* magazine. An anonymous ex-Moonie writes about the aftermath of her experience in the Unification Church (she was returned to her parents by the cult leaders after a mental breakdown): "Doctors diagnosed me as psychotic, out of touch with reality. Under the emotional and physical pressures of the cult, my mind 'just went.' It took months of intense treatment to put the pieces back together again. . . . Bills for my treatment came to more than $20,000; my parents will be paying for years" (p. 127).

In addition to forcible removal from a cult and separation by means of legal conservatorship, there is a third major way out of a cult — voluntary exit. Just how many young people leave extremist cults on their own initiative is impossible to ascertain. In most groups there appears to be some turnover during the first days and weeks of association, but nearly all ex-members report that the longer one is a part of a group, the more difficult it becomes to leave. Ex-members interviewed who had been abducted by their parents uniformly agree that they would never have left on their own. Whether or not that is a true assessment on their part is obviously unanswerable.

One former cultist told me that he left "because their rigorous life style was too much for me." An ex-member of ISKCON explained that he decided to leave because of health-related problems and because he was dissatisfied with the care his children were receiving. He also began to doubt the divinity of the spiritual master and the authority of the teachings he was exposed to. Nevertheless, he points out, "It was extremely difficult to leave the temple, because of the condemnation that one incurred. To leave the Hare Krishna movement was like committing spiritual suicide, because you were stepping into the snake pit when you left the temple."

A young man who left the Children of God on his own said that thoughts of an approaching Christmas season prompted him seriously to consider leaving. "I was very confused at that time in my life. I didn't know if I wanted to stay or leave. I finally left the colony about two weeks later. Coming out of the

Children of God was like going from one planet to another. And it was by no means a pleasant trip."

While the impact of destructive cults in our society is greatest upon the young people directly involved in them, the indirect emotional fallout upon parents reaches incalculable proportions. Marriages have been strained, financial resources depleted, and physical health impaired because a son or a daughter got involved in a cult. Several heart attacks and at least one parental death have been directly attributed to the extreme stress associated with attempts to rescue children from cults. The plight of the parents is sadly summarized by a mother who described her husband as "a totally broken man" while his daughter was a member of a cult. "You know that beautiful relationship that exists between a father and daughter? He was absolutely torn apart while she was gone. You could just see him dying an inch at a time, each day."

In a March 1977 case, unprecedented in American legal history, five families were granted temporary custody of their children by a California court in order to provide them with the opportunity to freely and voluntarily decide whether to continue their association with the Unification church. The young people, ranging in age from twenty-one to twenty-six, were the focus of an extended court hearing in which both sides made charges of "brainwashing." Responding to a plea by the attorney representing the youthful followers of Moon not to "turn them over to the wolves," the judge indicated that he trusted parents. "I know of no greater love than parents for their children, and I am sure they would not submit their children to harm."

◆ ELEVEN ◆

The Influence of
the Adversary

AS WE HAVE seen, historical, sociological, and psychological perspectives are valuable aids to any consideration of the current cult phenomenon. It is essential, however, to view the extremist groups from a Christian and biblical perspective in order to arrive at an explanatory framework in which all other explanations take on new significance.

I attempt here to delineate some of the determinants of cultic activity by using as a frame of reference the biblical doctrine of Satan. From the Christian perspective, the so-called new-age cults represent the most recent manifestation of an age-old struggle — the battle between good and evil, between God and God's adversary, Satan. The phenomena described in this book are neither random nor accidental: they are profoundly patterned. As simplistic as it may sound to some, they indicate a demonic conspiracy to subvert the true gospel of Jesus Christ through human agents whose minds have been blinded by the evil one.

In a secular and scientific age, it is not easy to discuss the reality of the demonic. For many people today, Satan is merely a figure of speech. According to the Roman Catholic scholar Nicolas Corte, "This very denial of the Devil on the part of a great number . . . is the surest sign of their subservience to him. He is the Father of lies, and there is no more deadly lie than the refusal to recognize his presence here in the very heart of human affairs" (Who Is the Devil? p. 118).

We are not talking about an abstract principle of evil, but a real and cosmic power. Jesus was thoroughly convinced of the existence of demons and the reality of Satan, as embarassing as this may be to contemporary man. In the sixth chapter of the Epistle to the Ephesians, the apostle Paul describes the kind of adversary with which we contend in the cults: "For our fight is not against any physical enemy: it is against organisations and powers that are spiritual. We are up against the unseen power that controls this dark world, and spiritual agents from the very headquarters of evil" (v. 12, *Phillips*).

The Greek term *diabolos*, or devil, is derived from a verb that means "to throw into confusion," "to upset," "to set at odds," "to put asunder." Satan's primary task is to come between God and mankind. In the particular case of the cults, Satan's strategy of producing confusion, discord, fear, and alienation has been well-documented. He has succeeded in separating parents from children, confusing and constricting the thinking of cult members, and subverting the wills of many sincere seekers. The influence of the adversary can be seen in so many ways in each of the cults we have considered. Typical of his working is the fact that Moonies come to believe that deception can be viewed as "heavenly," that the concept of "love" is radically redefined in the Love Family, and that the Hare Krishna devotee assumes the position that the human body created by God is nothing more than a "lump of ignorance" to be abhorred and abased.

Basic to the biblical view of God's adversary is the fact that he claims to be very religious. Throughout human history, Satan has time and again accomplished his purposes through existing forms of "religion." As the renowned German theologian Helmut Thielicke reminds us, the devil is a firm believer in God:

> That is why his disguise is so dangerous. For this reason is he so dangerous a seducer, a "teacher of error" in the Church, because there his principle of taking his stand on the fact of God, on the basis of positive Christian belief, is seen at its most effective. We may well say that the most diabiolical thing about the devil is that he takes this stand. That is why he is accounted a liar from the beginning. That is why he is called the "ape" of God. That is why we can mistake him for God (*Between God and Satan*, p. 31).

ALL THE groups we have studied use the word *church* or refer to deity in their formal identification or names: the Unification Church, the Children of God, the Church of Armageddon, the Way (Jesus referred to Himself as the way, the truth, and the life), and the Alamo Christian Foundation. In their recruitment of young people, the cults appear attractively religious, offering opportunities for Bible study, promises of secret or higher wisdom, and serious discussion of such lofty principles as love, truth, and God. How Satan can utilize such tactics is pointed out by Thielicke:

> What the devil means by God and the Son of God is not God at all, but a puppet whom the devil, to suit his own purposes, can cause to jump and dance and make bread and come down from his cross. This God is not Lord of the devil, but his slave. The devil uses him to turn to his own account the great things of life and to sanction them with his stolen name. . . . He uses him as a means of cementing and uniting men in the name of religion. . . . The devil does all this under cover of biblical and Christian phrases, and he can turn Christianity into a myth and an opiate in the same way (p. 35).

The adversary is a clever strategist, fully aware that people are vulnerable in that universal category of human experience — religion. The spiritual seduction we are witnessing today in the cults is certainly not a new phenomenon. The apostle Paul speaks to a quite similar situation in his letter to the churches in Galatia: "I am astonished to find you turning so quickly away from him who called you by grace, and following a different gospel. Not that it is in fact another gospel; only there are persons who unsettle your minds by trying to distort the gospel of Christ" (Gal. 1:6, 7, NEB). In the next verse Paul issues a harsh warning against those who attempt to pervert the gospel: "But even if we or an angel from heaven should preach a gospel other than the one we preached to you, let him be eternally condemned!" (v. 8, NIV).

It is noteworthy that Paul in this passage speaks of the minds of some young Christians being "unsettled" by false teachers. There are other specific references in his letters to the mind as being vulnerable to the influence of the adversary. Colossians 2:8 advises, "Be on your guard; do not let your minds be captured by hollow and delusive speculations, based on traditions of man-made teaching and centred on the elemental spirits of the universe and not on Christ" (NEB). In his first letter to Timothy, Paul writes, "The Spirit says expressly that in after times some will desert from the faith and give their minds to subversive doctrines inspired by devils, through the specious falsehoods of men whose own conscience is branded with the devil's sign" (4:1, NEB).

In *Your Adversary the Devil*, J. Dwight Pentecost states, "If Satan is to hold the minds and hearts of men captive to his lie, it is necessary for him to blind men to the truth as it is revealed in the Word of God" (p. 51). Scripture frequently uses the imagery of darkness or blindness to refer to the activity of the adversary vis-a-vis the minds of men and women. I suspect that the apostle Paul's writings would abound with such current terms as mind control, psychological and spiritual kidnaping, and brainwashing. In his second letter to the Corinthian Christians, Paul contrasts his own evangelistic approach with the deceptive methods of others who apparently sought to subvert the true Christian message. "We do not use deception, nor do we distort the word of God. On the contrary, by setting forth the truth plainly we commend ourselves to every man's conscience in the sight of God" (2 Cor. 4:2, NIV). In 2 Corinthians 4:4, he describes the work of the master of mind control: "The god of this age has blinded the minds of unbelievers, so that they cannot see the light of the gospel of the glory of Christ, who is the image of God."

As we have stated, a key to understanding the success of the extremist cults is the fact of their ability to destroy the will to be self-determining. In another book, Helmut Thielicke discusses this subversion of the will by the adversary who

> is also fond of using the instrument of *propaganda*, that is, nonobjective suggestion for the purpose of "forming the will." The very phrase "forming the will" is characteristic. For it indicates that propaganda does address itself to man as the bearer of a will, but nevertheless influences this will in such a secret and insinuating way that it is almost unconsciously changed and then accepts and carries out secretly imposed and suggested decisions as if they were its own (*Man in God's World*, p. 185).

PERSONS ACTIVE in the cults understandably do not perceive themselves as engaging in evil, nor do they see themselves as victims of deception. Their organizations and their leaders are upheld as paragons of truth, righteousness, and good works. But as Thielicke explains, "Through its diabolical obfuscating maneuvers the demonic power will always see to it that a person never feels that he is an *enemy of God* . . . but rather that he thinks he is acting in the *name of God*" (Ibid., p. 190).

The Bible teaches that spiritual counterfeits practice a "form of godliness" and that they do not always outwardly appear to be wrong. They usually, in fact, are very appealing. Scripture describes Satan as assuming the disguise of an "angel of light": "For such men are false apostles, deceitful workmen, masquerading as apostles of Christ. And no wonder, for Satan himself masquerades as an angel of light. It is not surprising, then, if his servants masquerade as servants of righteousness. Their end will be what their actions deserve" (2 Cor. 11:13–15, NIV).

False teachers not only imitate the real ministers of Christ, but regularly quote Scripture and distort the Bible for their own purposes. "The great seducer always uses the same devices: he seems to take God at his word, and yet he twists the meaning of this word almost before it has left God's mouth" (Thielicke, *Between God and Satan*, p. 55).

An example of this distortion of biblical teaching lies in the Children of God's use of two particular verses of Scripture to foster the alienation from parents that characterizes the extremist cults. All COG's have memorized the following Bible verses (from the King James Version): "If any man come to me, and hate not his father, and mother, and wife, and children, and brethren, and sisters, yea, and his own life also, he cannot be my disciple" (Luke 14:26); "And a man's foes shall be they of his own household" (Matt. 10:36).

The Children of God leaders take these verses out of context to support disdain for parents. But Christ did not advocate hatred of parents or family members. These verses illustrate the frequent use of hyperbole that characterized Christ's method of teaching; He was attempting to emphasize priorities and to show that no earthly relationship can be allowed to come before

God in the life of believers. To charge that Christ was teaching hatred of parents contradicts the biblical commandment to "honor thy father and thy mother" and creates the kind of confusion that delights Satan.

Certain members of the Children of God are referred to within the group as "10:36ers" in light of the COG interpretation of the Matthew passage. These members' interaction with their parents is restricted to occasional correspondence (with no return address) through a mail-drop. The parents are thereby prevented from knowing where their children are. According to the report of the New York State Attorney General's Office on COG activities, "When a '10:36' parent visits a commune, a signal is given and the commune goes into a 'security situation' and the child is secreted out of the commune. Meanwhile the parent is delayed by 'greeters' who tell the parent that either they never heard of the child or the child was elsewhere."

Such deceptive behavior can never be practiced by a true child of God. Ericson and MacPherson, in an article entitled, "The Deceptions of the Children of God," document the pattern of deceit and distortion that typifies this group. They cite an excerpt from a Mo letter as an example of how David Berg, the cult's founder, twists the teaching of the Bible:

> The Bible talks about obeying your parents in the Lord (which is your leadership, not your ungodly fleshly parents). It says obey them in all things, even if they are wrong! If a leader tells you to do something wrong you are justified before God for obeying leadership . . . (Christianity Today, July 20, 1973, p. 15).

In a Mo letter entitled "Public Relations," Berg gives his followers explicit instructions on how to deal with reporters: ". . . You can just *stall, evade, or lead* them off on another track. . . . Give them a good story. Try not to be negative in knocking the system, its churches, etc. — even public education! . . . It's OK to talk like this to each other, but not to outsiders!" (Ibid., p. 18). Ericson and MacPherson conclude,

> It is difficult to read and compare the various statements of David Berg and not conclude that they demonstrate a conscious pattern of deviousness. How this can be squared with the teachings of the Bible that Berg claims to venerate

we do not know. If Berg were to confess that he had been mistaken and overzealous in his past pronouncements and to promise to shift from deceptiveness to high Christian ethics, that would be one thing. Until he does, he stands exposed as practicing an unconscionable duplicity (p. 18).

Similar patterns of deception are observable in all the cult groups. The Moonies, for example, are quite content to misrepresent their cause for the sake of their ostensible ideal. They freely engage in "heavenly deception," because they feel that the overriding purpose of their mission is so great that they can lie to the existing world order because it is full of lies anyhow.

MOST CULT groups display great skill in using biblical language and Christian terminology. Even Eastern religious cults appeal to the Bible for support and affirmation by a selective use of texts that fit their own systems. Thielicke notes that when people misuse and exploit God's Word for ulterior purposes, then instead of being the Word of God, Scripture becomes a word of the adversary.

> That is why Jesus says to the people (Luke 6:46), "Why call ye me Lord, Lord, and do not the things that I say?" That means: You do indeed use pious words; you turn your eyes up to heaven, and seem to be on intimate terms with God; you talk the language of Canaan; you say "Lord, Lord" and "God says"; and yet all this is lies and a mean device of Satan. For you do not have the slightest idea what that word means, and thus you deprive it of all authority (Between God and Satan, p. 57).

The Mo letters of David Berg, the charter of the Church of Armageddon, the sermons of Reverend Moon — all contain quotations from Scripture, taken out of context and adapted to fulfill the purposes of the cults. "It is not God, but the Ape of God that speaks here — with words borrowed from the Lord himself" (Between God and Satan, p. 57).

The false prophets and self-appointed messiahs who head the cults belie the biblical model of leadership exemplified in Jesus Christ. Sun Myung Moon has stated to his followers: "I am a slave-driver to drive you out on a world mission." Referring to the founder and leader of ISKCON, Daner writes: "If the surface impressions of Bhaktivedanta lead one to think he is primarily sweetness and light, a closer look will illustrate how sharp is his demand on his followers and how great is their struggle to come closer to him. . . . The struggle and surrender to this spiritual master is harsh" (*The American Children of Krsna*, p. 20). By contrast, Jesus says, "Take my yoke upon you and learn from me, for I am gentle and humble in heart, and you will find rest for your souls. For my yoke is easy and my burden is light" (Matt. 11:29,30, NIV).

Many young people are attracted by the idealistic goals and ideologies proclaimed by the groups. We know, for example, that the Unification Church has lured large numbers of adherents through the promise of a better world, improved social conditions, and a united world religion — all to be achieved through massive human effort and a very regimented discipline of life. The influence of Satan can be seen in his efforts to subvert the inherent idealism of young people and redirect it to accommodate his own perverse ends.

Similarly the noble concepts of love, peace, truth, unity, and brotherhood — when disengaged from God and subverted by Satan — become empty and corrupted. Thielicke reiterates this principle when he states that "the great ideas and ideals of humanity, which may be of divine origin, are changed into their opposite the moment they are separated from their divine source" (*Man in God's World*, pp. 179–80).

FALSE PROPHETS are often sincere and full of humanitarian zeal. They are highly committed, and as we have pointed out, commitment is not inherently bad. In the extremist "high demand" cults we see commitment gone awry. Dr. John Mackay, former president of Princeton Seminary, is quoted as saying, "Commitment without reflection is fanaticism in action." The apostle Paul's warning concerning false teachers is strikingly contemporary: "Those people are zealous to win you over, but for no good. What they want is to alienate you from us, so that you may be zealous for them. It is fine to be zealous, provided the purpose is good . . ." (Gal. 4:17,18, NIV).

The devil always hides behind a mask; he never carries

an ID card. He employs rational, plausible, impressive methodologies and ideas. Ex-cult members often say something to the effect, "It all seemed so logical to me at the time; there was an answer for everything." Satan never offers to give people something evil; instead he offers individuals experiences that are ostensibly life-enriching. He offers power for abundant living, specialized knowledge and wisdom, and an opportunity to help convert the whole world.

It is Satan's design to subvert the very image of God in humanity at all levels at which people function, so as to conform them more to his image. The adversary is capable of subverting people's life styles in every respect, whether by philosophical justification, psychological influence, or direct spiritual influence. Diet, which is demonstrably related to the conditioning of consciousness and ultimately then to the altering of consciousness in a particular direction, may also be said to demonstrate the influence of the adversary.

Satan perverts or distorts what has been given by God to men and women for their blessing and benefit. Normal human activities like eating and sleeping, enjoyment, sex, leisure, aesthetics — all are subject to modification and interruption by Satan.

TO THE Christian observer, some cult groups are more directly involved in the realm of spiritualism, the occult-mystical, and the clearly demonic than other groups. The Moonies, for example, are almost preoccupied with the topic of Satan, the spirit world, and visionary experiences. On one occasion Reverend Moon shared the following with his disciples:

> The spirit world is to help you with your problems and help you with the Divine Principles, because I have already subjugated Satan on the spirit side. I have talked with many masters, including Jesus, on questions of life and the universe and creation, God's dispensation, and many other things. They have subjected themselves to me in terms of wisdom. After I won the victory, they surrendered. With this foundation of victory, the spirit world is responsible to teach and reply to your questions, and to help you with your problems.

In a question-and-answer session held during Moon's trip to

the United States in the spring of 1965, the leader of the Unification Church was asked about the significance of communicating with the spirits. He replied, "If you know the law of the spirit world and know how and why they can work with you, you can benefit from it." On another occasion during the same visit he made these revealing comments:

> The whole spirit world is under your Leader.... Without the unification of the spirit world, which is the world of cause or origin, you could never have the Divine Principle. Sensitives or mediums, who do not know the basic principles, becomes slaves of the spirit world and are apt to meet tragic ends. . . . Many sensitives who have not seen me in person have seen me in my spirit. There are many who are now directly led by me.

A number of my interviewees reported having unusual mystical experiences while they were members of various cults. Some have become Christians since leaving the cults and now attribute these events to demonic activity. An ex-ISKCON member describes his first contact with a Hare Krishna devotee: "As he sat there, I could feel something in my body, my person. I could sense in some wonderful way his very presence next to me by means of a slight, warm tingling feeling. That young man might as well have glowed in the dark before me, the light shined on him so remarkably that day. As I now see it, he no doubt shined under the influence of spirits."

The same person continues, "There were spiritual forces involved — tugging and pulling and encouraging and framing me up in every possible way. I was set up like a bowling pin for this whole thing. Now I see my whole experience as being just saturated with the presence of demonic beings influencing me with signs and wonders. Subtle changes were wrought in my mind and heart and thinking by the spirits that stood behind the ISKCON doctrine and the group that was trying to draw me in."

Several former cultists relate bizarre experiences in connection with meditating or chanting. "All I wanted to do was chant. I had, through surrender, accepted a spirit that needed to feed and satisfy itself through that activity. The more I got into it, the more that spirit found expression through me. The effect of the chanting itself was a remarkable encounter with spirits. You begin to chant and you can feel a cloud sort of settle over you. It was a numbing kind of experience; you felt rather locked in or tuned in to what you were doing. It feels very much like a marijuana high: everything becomes rather dull and you become kind of satiated by the whole experience so that the world with its problems doesn't really matter.

"All of this was caused by a spirit of false peace which was later cast out of my person. I felt that cloud lift, and my eyes were truly opened in a wonderful way at the moment when the spirit was cast from my body. What was pulling me and encouraging me and granting me these feelings were actually living spirits of a very specific sort."

An ex-Moonie remembers seeing a young man reported to be demon possessed. "I still don't know if it was possession or if he was temporarily insane, but it all happened very suddenly. He spoke with another voice and didn't sound like himself at all. He had tremendous strength. It took about ten people to hold him down. When it subsided, he didn't remember anything. He was so remorseful and so sad. They kicked him out of the movement because they felt that he had been opened to the spiritual world." This incident brings to mind the question raised in the third chapter of Mark's Gospel: "How can Satan cast out Satan?"

While such psychospiritual phenomena may be far removed from the experience of most Americans, there are increasing numbers of people who have been experientially convinced of the existence of dimensions of reality extending beyond the merely physical. The emergence of the new-age cults must, in fact, be viewed against the historical background of developments in Western culture and thought since 1960.

THE ORGANIZATION that has done the most penetrating and biblically insightful analysis of historical trends in Western thought as they relate to contemporary cults is the Spiritual Counterfeits Project, a ministry of the Berkeley Christian Coalition. A primary purpose of the Spiritual Counterfeits Project (SCP) is to research the major occult, psychic, and mystical spiritual groups existing in America today and to critique those groups biblically. The analysis presented here is in large part indebted to the insights provided by the staff members of this organization.

According to SCP researchers, the United States is currently witnessing the impact of a major transformation of the general consciousness of Western society that has its roots, in part, in the emergence of the countercultural, occult spiritual community associated with the alternative youth culture beginning in the mid-1960s. "There is little question that the occult philosophical underpinnings of much of the counterculture are becoming increasingly infused into mainstream thought and are transforming it" ("A Preliminary Blueprint for Discernment," SCP pamphlet).

The psychedelic revolution and the phenomenal popularity of Eastern mystical religions set the stage for the appearance on the American scene of the extremist cults we have examined. The research of Dr. Daner and other behavioral scientists clearly indicates that prior psychedelic drug experiences of cult members paves the way for participation in new-age religious groups. Entrance into such groups frequently represents a desire to escape an unfulfilling "hippie" life and to experience another form of consciousness alteration that bypasses drugs altogether. In addition to drugs, experimentation with such things as vegetarian diets, Transcendental Meditation, sexual permissiveness, travel, and Eastern philosophies appear to be contributing factors.

According to a recent Gallup poll, some six million Americans meditate, five million practice yoga, and two million are deeply into formal Eastern religions. The cover story of the November 6, 1976 issue of *Newsweek* was devoted to the consciousness revolution that is sweeping America. This pervasive movement represents an admixture of modern Western psychotherapy with the ancient disciplines of Eastern religions. Millions of Americans are exploring and experiencing various body therapies, est (Erhard Seminars Training), Silva Mind Control, TM, primal therapy, and a host of other techniques for expanding consciousness and enhancing mystical experiences. According to *Newsweek*, the consciousness movement "is a religion without a creed, a catalyst for new lifestyles, a tournament of therapies in which powerful gurus joust for converts even as they press forward in their cultic quest for self-transcendence" (p. 56).

All this evidence points to the conclusion that there is a cultural predisposition in American society that facilitates the entry of increasing numbers of young people into extremist cults. All this indicates the influence of the adversary:

> We can see that the enormous current popularity of TM, est, and yoga is a direct symptom of the influence of the occult spiritual community. When Maharishi first brought TM to America in the early sixties, it bombed. The need for relaxation was the same, but people just weren't ready to hear about "meditation" as a remedy for stress. Today, however, TM is virtually a household word, particularly in America. And through it, Satan has almost succeeded in establishing a "vision of possibilities" particularly suited to the mainstream cultural predisposition ("A Preliminary Blueprint for Discernment," SCP pamphlet).

CLEARLY, THE adversary cannot be conquered by men and women. His ultimate defeat will come at the hands of the Lord of the universe, God Himself. Until then, what is to be the response of the church and the individual Christian to the onslaught of the cults?

In suggesting an answer to this vital question, I should like to present a modified version of the stated objectives of the Spiritual Counterfeits Project, because these purposes deserve consideration within the whole Christian community:

1. To equip Christians to understand the sociopsychological, philosophical, and spiritual dimensions of the contemporary cult explosion;
2. To suggest, on this basis, a Christian response that wields the sword of His truth as a life-saving scalpel. Knowledge always implies responsibility. There is a need for the body of Christ to issue a strong prophetic warning to the secular society;
3. To extend a hand of rescue to the psychically and spiritually molested. This means —
   a. Approaching them where they are by entering into their system of belief. We must care enough to comprehend

fully the "question" before offering an answer;
b. Revealing the captivity of those who think they are free. They must be shown the inconsistencies, neglected questions, and constricted perspectives of their own philosophies in their own terms;
c. Offering an avenue of escape via the gospel of Jesus Christ. By caring enough to understand, we express the concern that motivates evangelism in the first place. In this way we truly become all things to all people without compromising the strength and integrity of the gospel.

The approach of the Spiritual Counterfeits Project is holistic. It attempts to treat "cultism" within the larger frame of reference of an analysis of the whole of Western life and thought. That is a large order. The Christian academic community can play a significant role in achieving that objective.

> We believe that it is vital to recognize that the very influences which are at the root of the Western cultural predisposition to embrace Eastern/occult metaphysics have been steadily gaining acceptance as cherished premises upon which rests much of the expression of contemporary (ostensible) "Christianity." *It will do very little good for the Church to confront the cults unless we simultaneously confront our own participation in the conditions which have produced them.* The ultimate spiritual counterfeit is a Christianity which has been squeezed so far into the world's mold that all distinguishing authenticity has been squeezed out of it — a Christianity which is culturally co-opted, socially irrelevant, doctrinally correct and spiritually dead (*Spiritual Counterfeits Project Newsletter*, September 1976, p. 5).

Such a perspective requires that the church be the church, that it be honest about its complacency and failure to provide a living and visible alternative to destructive cults. The spiritual quest of hundreds of thousands of American youth indicts our society as a whole, but it raises urgent questions for the church in particular. Young people are highly idealistic; many have rejected the materialistic sham that passes for the "good life" in America. Is the church speaking to the gross materialism of Western society, or has it co-opted? Young people are asking the big questions — but are the churches providing more than fun-and-games youth programs in response? Is the church assisting youth to raise the right questions and then providing the resources for arriving at meaningful, biblically based answers? Have we wisely and purposefully enlisted the energies and enthusiasm of young men and women? Have we equipped them with a solid doctrinal base from which to counter the wiles of the adversary?

Parents both within and outside the Christian community must be willing to admit the inadequacies and weak spots in our family functioning. While it is appropriate to recognize that the larger society has made devastating inroads upon the institution of the family, it is equally important to remember that individual parents bear major responsibility for providing a structured environment and an atmosphere of genuine concern and love. A home situation in which a young person perceives a lack of understanding, an inability to listen, or a failure to respect the opinions and values of youth is vulnerable to the supplanting tactics of the cults.

Young people are attracted to cults for various reasons. As one ex-member observes, "It offers you a place where you are accepted; you have a structure; you know what is expected of you and you are respected. You have a place, you have a position; you feel part of an honorable thing; you have meaning and purpose in your life." Though the structure may consist of an unhealthy authoritarianism or a rigid puritanicalism, it is more structure than a permissive society provides. Though the acceptance may be tied to an exploitative usefulness to the group, it is perhaps more acceptance than is available in many of our schools and other bureaucratic institutions. Though the activities of the cult may be fraudulent and anything but "honorable," in a perverted kind of way the member is made to feel that he/she is important and that the purposes of the organization are noble and honorable. In short, young people need acceptance, structure, clear-cut goals and values, a feeling of self-worth, and recognition that they are valuable contributors to the community and to the society. In this the cults present a challenge to the institutions of our society — the family, the schools, the churches and synagogues, the political and economic structures — to take heed.

CHRISTIANS MUST be careful to respond constructively rather than react frantically to the new-age cults. There has been a tendency in some circles to mount an anti-cult crusade, which can only result in frustration and being outmaneuvered by the adversary. It should always be remembered that "our fight is not against any physical enemy: it is against organisations and powers that are spiritual" (Eph. 6:12, *Phillips*). An unthinking confrontative stance vis-à-vis the cults can easily foster "a witch-hunt mentality among zealous Christians who naively identify the main thrust of Satan's work as being in and through the cults, while ignoring the equally destructive seductions of other aspects of the 'world system'" (*SCP Newsletter*, September 1976).

The victims of mind control must be approached in genuine Christian love. We should always distinguish between the person who has been victimized and the power that holds him in the cult. The apostle Paul, writing to Timothy, describes the model attitude of "the Lord's servant": "Those who oppose him he must gently instruct, in the hope that God will give them a change of heart leading them to a knowledge of the truth, and that they will come to their senses and escape from the trap of the devil, who has taken them captive to do his will" (2 Tim. 2:25,26, NIV).

Paul's injunction to be "gentle" is especially appropriate for the person who has just come out of a destructive cult. In the words of an ex-member whose story is told in the first part of the book, many are suffering from "an overdose of religion." The Christian church has an opportunity to be truly redemptive in dealing with ex-cultists. Christians have led the way in providing help for those people in our society who have had unfortunate life experiences with alcohol and drug abuse. Currently there is a need for informed, concerned Christians to provide counseling and other supportive services for ex-cultists — perhaps following the "half-way house" model. There is reason to believe that a sizable number of young people want to leave the cults — provided there is a haven of refuge for them.

We must continually be alert to the activity of the evil one. "Watch out for false prophets. They come to you in sheep's clothing, but inwardly they are ferocious wolves. By their fruit you will recognize them" (Matt. 7:15,16, NIV). At the same time, we must not be so preoccupied with the devil that we fail to emphasize the victory of Jesus Christ. "The energy of the Church can be diverted into a polemic against 'evil' without a corresponding development of 'the good' of the Kingdom" (SCP Newsletter, September 1976). "For Satan must not be allowed to get the better of us; we know his wiles all too well" (2 Cor. 2:11, NEB).

Christ is here! He is Victor! He is Liberator! "So if the Son sets you free, you will be free indeed" (John 8:36, NIV).

◆ BIBLIOGRAPHY ◆

Books

Daner, Francine Jeanne. *The American Children of Krsna.* New York: Holt, Rinehart and Winston, 1976.

Enroth, Ronald M.; Ericson, Edward E.; and Peters, C. Breckinridge. *The Jesus People.* Grand Rapids: Wm. B. Eerdmans Publishing Co., 1972.

Kanter, Rosabeth Moss. *Commitment and Community.* Cambridge, Mass.: Harvard University Press, 1972.

Lifton, Robert J. *Thought Reform and the Psychology of Totalism.* New York: W. W. Norton and Company, 1961.

Pentecost, J. Dwight. *Your Adversary the Devil.* Grand Rapids: Zondervan Publishing House, 1969.

Thielicke, Helmut. *Between God and Satan.* Grand Rapids: Wm. B. Eerdmans Publishing Co., 1958.

_____. *Man in God's World.* New York: Harper and Row, 1963.

Zablocki, Benjamin. *The Joyful Community.* Baltimore: Penguin Books, 1971.

Articles and Periodicals

Edwards, Charles H. "How I Rescued My Son from the Moonies." *Medical Economics,* 1 November 1976, pp. 73-80.

Ericson, Edward E., and MacPherson, Paul. "The Deceptions of the Children of God." *Christianity Today,* 20 July 1973, pp. 14-20.

"Getting Your Head Together." *Newsweek,* 6 September 1976, pp. 56-72.

Gunther, Max. "Brainwashing: Persuasion by Propaganda." *Today's Health,* February 1976, pp. 15ff.

Moore, Thomas. "Where Have All the Children of God Gone?" *New Times,* October 1974, pp. 32-41.

Rasmussen, Mark. "How Sun Myung Moon Lures America's Children." *McCall's,* September 1976, pp. 102ff.

Rice, Berkeley. "Honor Thy Father Moon." *Psychology Today,* January 1976, pp. 36ff.

Richardson, James T.; Harder, Mary; and Simmonds, Robert. "Thought Reform and the Jesus Movement." *Youth and Society,* December 1972, pp. 102ff.

Sage, Wayne. "The War on the Cults." *Human Behavior,* October 1976, pp. 40-49.

Spiritual Counterfeits Project Newsletter, September 1976.

◆ INDEX ◆